Be Your Own Spin Doctor

Praise for the first edition of *Be Your Own Spin Doctor:*

The god-like genius of Paul Richards
The title may be opportunistic, but behind the gloss and the name-dropping is a book that provides everything the spin doctors don't want you to know. Drawing on his own experiences, the man who as Labour candidate for Billericay managed to get *Newsnight* to a Labour Party plant sale, helps you understand how journalists work and teaches that dealing with the media is a skill not magic – 'there are tricks of the trade and techniques that can be learnt'.

Labour Left Briefing

Richards has an acerbic turn of phrase and a good line in anecdotes ... Impressive.

Sunday Telegraph

My only motive for plugging this book is that it is worth reading ... *Be Your Own Spin Doctor* is punchy, clear and well laid out.

Phil Woolas MP

I am going to urge every colleague and friend in every organisation devoted to returning the centre-left to its democratic socialist traditions to go out, buy a copy, read it and act upon it.

Tim Pendry, Chartist

A useful guide to good practice in public relations and news management.

Labour Organiser

A valuable insight into what needs to be done when dealing professionally with the press.

David Hill

Fabulous.

Tribune

Be Your Own Spin Doctor
A Practical Guide to Using the Media

Paul Richards

'A useful guide for all campaigners and communicators.'

Peter Mandelson

POLITICO'S

First edition published in 1998 by Take That Publishing

This edition published in 2005 by Politico's Publishing, an imprint of
Methuen Publishing
11–12 Buckingham Gate
London SW1E 6LB

www.politicos.co.uk/publishing

10 9 8 7 6 5 4 3 2 1

A catalogue record for this book is available from the British Library.

ISBN 1 84275 136 0

Printed and bound in Great Britain by The St. Edmundsbury Press.

Typeset in Garamond by Duncan Brack.

Contents

About the Author

Paul Richards is an author, journalist and campaigner. In August 2005 he was appointed as Special Adviser at the Department of Health, working for Secretary of State Patricia Hewitt MP.

As director of Paul Richards Communications Limited, he has provided advice and training to a variety of organisations in the not-for-profit, trade union, public and charity sectors, including the Communication Workers Union, GMB, Cancer Research UK, Alzheimer's Society, Community Service Volunteers (CSV), Big Lottery Fund and the Neighbourhood Renewal Unit in the Office of the Deputy Prime Minister (ODPM).

Since 2000 he has worked with local not-for-profit groups in Birmingham, Brighton, Bristol, Bradford, Cardiff, Chester, Coventry, Darlington, Doncaster, Exeter, Hull, Hartlepool, Leeds, Leicester, Liverpool, London, Newcastle, Nottingham, Norwich, Oldham, Manchester, Rochdale, Sheffield, Wolverhampton and York. He has also run training courses in communications for public-sector officials from Eritrea, Ethiopia, Ghana, Gambia, Indonesia, Malaysia, Nigeria, and Tanzania.

His first book was the first edition of *Be Your Own Spin Doctor – A Practical Guide to Using the Media* (1998), which was a Politico's bestseller for several years. In 2001 his second book, *How to Win an Election – The Art of Political Campaigning,* was published, with a new updated edition in 2004. He is the author of several political pamphlets, including *Long to Reign Over Us?* (1996), *Is the Party Over?* (2000) and *The Case for Socialism* (2000).

He is the editor of a collection of speeches and articles by the Prime Minister, *Tony Blair: In His Own Words,* published by Politico's in 2004.

As a journalist, Paul has written for a variety of newspapers and magazines and has appeared on radio and television. He has been interviewed by Jeremy Paxman, John Humphreys, Clive Anderson, and Kirsty Wark, and he has appeared on Radio 4's *Today* and *The Moral Maze*, BBC TV's *Newsnight*, and *This Morning* on ITV. Paul has given lectures to journalism students at City University, the London College of Communication, and Cardiff University's school of journalism. His first job was as an unpaid trainee reporter on the *Buckinghamshire Advertiser* in 1984.

He has been a Labour Party parliamentary candidate twice – in Billericay in 1997 and in Lewes in 2001. He was chair of the Fabian Society from 2002 to 2003. Until 2005 he worked part-time for Hazel Blears, MP for Salford.

Paul Richards is married to Sarah, and they have one son, Alexander. They live in Southfields in south-west London.

Acknowledgements

I'd like to thank Emma Carr for her research, Ellie Levenson, Sean Magee, Emma Musgrave, Duncan Brack, and all at Politico's, John Schwartz, Lorraine Eames, and all the people, too numerous to list here, who offered their comments on *Be Your Own Spin Doctor* since it first appeared in 1998.

This book is dedicated to Sarah, whose wonderfulness needs no spin.

Introduction to the new edition
Living in Spin

How the world has changed since 1998, when *Be Your Own Spin Doctor* was first published. Britannia was Cool, Pop was Brit, Labour was New, and we were all much younger back then. Peter Mandelson even came to the launch party. The phrase 'spin doctor' carried with it a little edginess, a touch of intrigue, and more than a dose of fascination. In under a decade 'spin' has been devalued and debased through an endless procession of exposés, investigations, and official inquiries.

Today, the phrase 'spin doctor' is derogatory – it ranks alongside mugger, drugs dealer, or estate agent in public esteem. What was once a byword for sharp practice and cynical media manipulation has become, for some, the cause of all that is wrong with politics and public life. A light-hearted Christmas television programme in 2004 even named ex-spin doctor Jo Moore, of 'good day to bury bad news' notoriety, as the 'second most reviled woman in Britain'. Second most reviled woman. Behind Myra Hindley, Beverley Allitt, or Rosemary West?

Spin, it seems, is bad news.

I considered whether to give the new edition of this book the same title as the first. Would mention of the dreaded 'spin' put people off? Would it create confusion or, worse, hostility? People told me it was a bad idea, but what do they know? I decided that we would publish under the original title, and be damned.

The title needs some explanation. Spin doctoring is a relatively new expression used to describe a very old practice. People with a story have always tried to find the best way to tell it. We do it when we apply for a job and get interviewed, when we try to sell our house or car, or when we go on a first date. Only a fool lies about their accomplishments because even the most plausible and adept liars are found out; but we don't exactly draw attention to our failings and weaknesses either. We accentuate the positive, and ignore, obfuscate or camouflage the negatives. We spin.

Spin is older than radio, older than television, even older than printing. It started when the first early human strung a sentence together for the very first time. The world's religions rely on spin doctors – the priests, imams, vicars, rabbis and others who present their faith in the best possible light. Anyone trying to sell us something, from cars to holidays to cans of soup, needs to advertise its best points. Anglers know a thing or two about spin – just ask them about the one that got away. The ancient Greeks and Romans understood that the truth was not enough – it needed packaging and presentation, and so the art of rhetoric was developed. Politicians, visionaries, revolutionaries, social reformers – all have used what today we dismiss as spin. Lenin didn't sit at his desk in the Zurich public library and daydream about revolution – he created a newspaper and an army of spin doctors and sent them out to the Russian masses with his famous sound bite: 'bread, peace and land'. Florence Nightingale used the media to win support for extra supplies from a hard-hearted War Office. Even Jesus Christ knew a thing or two about communications – the need for eye-catching stunts, effective presentation, simple sound bites and memorable stories. He called them parables.

Why has so much attention been given to spin in the past few years? What has changed in recent decades is neither the need for spin, nor in many ways the practice of spin. What has changed is the explosion of the 24/7 media. Anyone wanting to communicate a message to millions cannot rely on word of mouth, and most cannot afford to advertise. So spin has developed as a direct result of the explosion of media – newspapers, magazines, television and radio, and online.

Anyone who, like me, was born in the 1960s can remember a Britain where there were only three television channels, which had to be changed by standing up and walking to the set, where television programmes came to a stop before midnight with the national anthem and an announcer telling you to unplug your television, and where 'daytime TV' consisted of a small girl playing noughts and crosses with a toy clown for hours on end. The arrival of remote controls, Channel 4, video recorders, breakfast news, Sky, and now DVDs and digital television has happened within our lifetimes.

The way we consume our media has changed. 'Breakfast news' used to mean a national newspaper read over tea and toast at the family kitchen table. Now it might mean a look at the *Daily Mirror*, *The Times* or *The Guardian*, but it is far more likely to mean Sky News, or GMTV, or *Today* on Radio 4, or local radio in the car, or a download of news from the internet on to your palmtop or phone, or a glance at your favourite news blog. Even since the publication of *Be Your Own Spin Doctor,* in 1998, the numbers of people getting news and information online, or on their mobile phones, has dramatically increased. And 'blog' back then meant nothing.

The media, and the ways in which we consume it, has become more diverse and more personalised, and is available 24 hours a day. 'News' is not a programme, it is the permanent output on a series of channels. It does not happen at a set time, it is all the time. So naturally the style, pace and approach of today's spin doctor has to keep up with the relentless rollercoaster of rolling news.

Anyone serious about selling their message cannot rely on the occasional lunch with a newspaper editor or the odd news release. Building, maintaining and protecting a celebrity, corporate or political reputation is a full-time job, reflective of the insatiable demand for news and comment from an increasingly diverse media. The explosion of media means that there are more opportunities for spin: more news outlets that need feeding, more interview slots that need filling, more experts that need providing, and more space for your message. Like the plant in *Little Shop of Horrors*, the endless refrain is 'feed me'.

The premise for this book, and what I am told made it useful to its readers first time round, is that all of us can be spin doctors if we have a cause we want to promote, an issue we want to raise, or a campaign we want to kick-start. The techniques of the White House, Downing Street, St James's Palace and Square Mile spin doctors can be used to support the save the local hospital campaign, sell tickets for the am-dram production of *The Mikado*, raise funds for your local scout troop, regenerate your neighbourhood, or plug your new website, charity, book or small business.

The reason is simple: the way we perceive the world beyond our immediate personal experience is shaped by the media; the media is shaped by spin; and spin can be provided by you. So what follows is not a guide to the black arts of manipulation and subterfuge, nor tips on lying and deceit, but some practical advice on how to influence the media in all its forms and get your message across. One reviewer of the first edition on the Amazon website wrote:

> I read it hoping to find out how to manipulate the press and to force people to vote for things they really don't want. Instead the book is a relatively down-to-earth guide to handling the media and being a press officer. How disappointing.

I hope you won't be disappointed by what follows. If your voice deserves to be heard, neither an absence of knowledge about how to reach a wider audience via the media nor the lack of funds to hire a professional should be a barrier. This little book shows you how to be your own spin doctor.

Paul Richards
London
June 2005

We should put the spin doctors in the spin clinics, where they can meet other spin patients and be treated by spin consultants. Then the rest of us can get on with the proper democratic process.

Tony Benn

The latest spin is: there is no spin.

Armando Iannucci

Chapter One
In Defence of Spin

If you've done it, it ain't braggin'.

Dizzy Dean, US baseball player

Let us start by defining our terms.

Ask the man or woman on the Clapham Omnibus about 'spin' and 'spin doctors' and you will get a strongly negative reaction. Most people feel uneasy with the idea, and have wrapped it up in their own minds with 'propaganda', 'manipulation', 'cheating', 'lying' or 'public relations'. But when asked for a definition, the same people fail to come up with one. People know that spin is a bad thing, but don't know what it is.

So how might we define spin? Melanie Phillips, writing in *The Observer* on 12 October 1997, after a few months of Labour government, called spin doctoring 'a package of trickery, economies with the truth, manipulation of public credulity, bullying of journalists and favouritism'.

A Gallup survey for the *Daily Telegraph* showed that in the minority of cases where people knew what a spin doctor was, terms such as 'liar', 'charlatan', 'manipulator', and 'con artist' were most commonly applied. Definitions included: 'someone who phones out the gossip to the papers', 'a devious person' and 'somebody who finds great difficulty in telling the truth' and who 'gives off a lot of hot air and is paid a lot of money'.

That negative image is not helped by people like Michael Shea, whose political thriller *Spin Doctor* describes these modern Machiavellis as:

> ... professional political strategists, able on behalf of their clients to manipulate the media – planting a story here, a rumour there, a tip-off somewhere else – so that any piece of news is tailored to show them in the best possible light.

The opening act in Shea's novel sees a woman being framed with heroin dealing by the spin doctor, after threatening to embarrass a Tory minister. Not a particularly helpful portrayal.

Ken Follett, the novelist and husband of a Labour MP, goes further:

> People who do the briefing, who whisper words of poison into the ears of journalists, are of no consequence. They are the rent boys of politics, and we shudder with disgust when they brush past us in the corridor.

The *Chambers 21st Century Dictionary* defines spin doctor as:

> Someone, especially in politics, who tries to influence public opinion by putting a favourable bias on information presented to the public or to the media.

The *Concise Oxford English Dictionary* suggests a spin doctor is:

> A spokesperson for a political party or person employed to give a favourable interpretation of events to the media.

These dictionary definitions get us some of the way there. It is right to highlight the realm of politics in the development of spin doctoring, but spin is far from confined to politicians. Most major organisations employ spin doctors: businesses, charities, celebrities, campaigns, even countries. In August 2004, the papers were full of tales of a botched spin operation by the Football Association (about which more later). We've known about the Queen's spin doctors for two decades or more. And what about the Civil Service, the Army, Tesco, Virgin Rail, British American Tobacco, Nokia and Friends of the Earth – don't they employ spin doctors too?

What about this idea of putting a 'favourable bias' or 'favourable interpretation' on information? Is putting a favourable bias on things confined to spin doctors? Isn't that what every job interviewee, contractor pitching for business, or first-time dater is doing all the time? Who puts an unfavourable bias on what they say about themselves? The American writer Alan Harrington says that public relations is 'the craft of arranging the truth so that people like you'.

With this definition, spin is no more morally reprehensible or responsible for the downfall of public standards than the market trader who puts the fresh apples at the front of his stall, and hides the bruised ones at the back.

And what about journalists? Don't they write and broadcast their own spin on things? Aren't the professional choices they make subject to their own convictions, views, prejudices, upbringing, and proprietorial influence? Don't they choose to give a voice to certain points of view and perspectives which mirror their own view of the world, or the editorial line of their publication? If journalists were simply reflectors of a perfect, objective truth, then the *Daily Mail* and *The Guardian* would be full of the same stories, written in the same way, every day of the week. As Alastair Campbell wrote in the *Mirror* on 3 July 2000, 'the vast bulk of spin comes from what I call journalist spin doctors'.

The term spin doctor was born, along with many of the techniques, in the United States of America. Spin doctor is an amalgam of 'spin' – the interpretation or slant placed on events (which is a sporting metaphor, taken from the spin put on a baseball by the pitcher, or the spin put on the cue-ball in pool) – and 'doctor', deriving from the figurative uses of the word to mean 'patch up', 'piece together', and 'falsify'. The phrase first appeared in print in the *New York Times* during the 1984 US presidential election, and during the 1980s the term became common amongst the political classes on both sides of the Atlantic, especially during the 1988 US presidential election.

In Britain, the term is often applied to the handful of 'special advisers' employed by government politicians. But not all special advisers are spin doctors. Most of the 80-odd special advisers employed by government ministers are policy experts whose day-to-day work involves meetings with civil servants and interest groups, drafting policy documents and speeches, and providing another perspective and political advice to ministers otherwise reliant on the civil service. These special advisers have few, if any, dealings with the media beyond occasional phone briefings and ghost-writing articles. In March 2002, the then Cabinet Secretary Sir Richard Wilson pointed out that there were 81 special advisers in government, of whom 11 were media relations specialists. At the same time there were 3,429 senior civil servants, and about 400,000 civil servants in total. Even Tony Blair was moved to remark: 'I think we need to get this in context.'

So what is a spin doctor? A spin doctor is a media specialist, with an expert knowledge and understanding of journalism and journalists, who uses his or her professional skills to help an organisation or individual get a message across to the right people. The spin doctor's role is a highly skilled job, requiring a higher level of credibility and expertise than possessed by a press officer or public relations officer. These jobs, though perfectly respectable and useful, are more concerned with drafting and issuing news releases and answering factual enquiries. The press officer is to the spin doctor what the first violin is to the orchestra's conductor. On this definition, it is obvious that spin doctors exist far beyond the narrow bear pit of politics.

Spin doctors are people employed for their skills at communicating. They can advise their bosses or organisations on how to present a positive face to the world, how to harness the awesome power of the mass media, how to avoid making the kind of mistakes which can send the share price into free-fall or cause the snap resignation. The modern spin doctor is not a liar, or a dissembler, or a fraudster, or a manipulator – he or she is an invaluable asset to an organisation, and, much to the chagrin of journalists, an important contributor to the world of journalism. After hours of hearings and mountains of evidence, the Hutton Inquiry into the government's use of spin to sell its message that Saddam Hussein represented a danger to Britain could find no actual lies that had been told by Alastair Campbell or any other government spin doctor. The only person blamed for telling lies was ex-BBC journalist Andrew Gilligan, for pretending that he knew more than he did. Such is the terrible reputation of spin doctoring that when the Hutton Inquiry exonerated Campbell, and failed to find any evidence of lying, many people dismissed it as 'whitewash'.

In the age of modern communications, the spin doctor has become an invaluable link between leaders in business, politics, public life or celebrities and the consumers of media (that's you and me). It is through the media – newspapers, radio, television, and internet – that we view the world beyond our immediate environment. In an age where no one attends public meetings to hear speeches, or digests lengthy policy manifestos or a business prospectus, it is through the media that our reality is created. Those who can use the media to their advantage can effectively shape reality.

The growth of spin doctoring is shown in the expansion of the public relations business. The Institute for Public Relations (IPR) puts the number of people employed in PR in the UK at over 50,000, with PR consultancies turning over a billion pounds a year. Sixteen UK universities and colleges offer PR as an undergraduate degree.

Spin is big business.

The truth is a difficult concept

Spin doctors exist because there is no such thing as an objective truth. As Justice Scott concluded after his inquiry into the Matrix Churchill scandal, 'the truth is a difficult concept'. Socialist MP Aneurin Bevan was fond of challenging his interlocutors with the demand: 'that's my truth – now tell me yours'.

Facts, figures, events, words – all have different meanings to different people. Interpretation is the key. A famous television advertisement a few years ago for *The Guardian* showed a skinhead running towards a businessman in the street. We assume the skinhead is a mugger, but actually he saves the businessman from falling masonry. The information presented to us plays on one set of prejudices and leads us to make a set of assumptions, but the extra information turns our view by 360 degrees.

In February 2005, former Labour MP and television presenter Robert Kilroy-Silk launched a new political party, Veritas (Latin for 'truth'), with a promise to end the 'lies and spin'. On the day he launched Veritas, the BBC reported Mr Kilroy-Silk as claiming that 'our country' was 'being stolen' by mass immigration. So whose truth was that? Despite many people's fears and misconceptions, only around 10 per cent of the British population can be considered 'immigrants' and the Home Office reckons that immigrants contribute 10 per cent more in taxes to the British economy than they take in benefits. As Tory MP Tony Baldry told the BBC: 'Anyone reading the British press might assume that the UK is in the front line of dealing with migrants and refugees. This is simply wrong.' So in its first hours of existence Veritas fell far from its vaunted aims of 'truth', and descended into the worst kind of political rabble-rousing.

In famously declaring that 'the medium is the message', the communications guru Marshall McLuhan suggested that it is not only what you say, but how, where and when you say it that is important. That means that the way you say something is as critical as what you say. Political parties try to look hip and happening by sending out SMS text messages to young people. Music promoters try to flog CDs by making their advertising look like urban graffiti.

The remarkably fresh television comedy *Yes, Minister*, written in the late 1970s and early 1980s about a fictional politician, contains memorable advice from a spin doctor on how to run a television broadcast:

> If you're changing a lot of things, you want to look reassuring and traditional. Therefore you should have a dark suit and an oak-panelled background and leather books. But if you're not doing anything new, you'd want a light modern suit and a modern high-tech setting with abstract paintings.

And as for the music? 'Bach for new ideas; Stravinsky for no change.'

The TV illusionist Derren Brown is a master of manipulation through his use of word association, suggestion, subliminal signalling and old-fashioned misdirection. There is nothing magic about what he does. He is skilled at reading people's reactions and knowing how most people behave in a given situation. He knows what words will plant ideas in people's minds without them realising. The spin doctor is the equivalent of the TV illusionist. Spin is about knowing which words and phrases will have what impact, how people will react when hearing them, how the brain receives visual and verbal information, and how journalists will behave in set scenarios.

The businessman wearing a sober suit and modest tie interviewed in a book-lined office with a picture of his wife on the desk already commands authority and respect, even if he is the biggest crook since Richard Nixon.

The politician faced by journalists asking about an affair with his secretary, who rushes into his car and hurriedly drives off, already looks as though he has something to hide. The errant government minister photographed hiding his face in the back seat of a speeding car looks guilty as sin.

A politician hit by a sex scandal who appears with his entire family – wife, progeny, parents, in-laws and all – at the garden gate of the family home, and offers the press pack tea and biscuits, is already speaking volumes about their family values (regardless of the reality).

We may like to feel that we are immune to such nonsense, and can see through subliminal messages, subtle hints, and word associations, but the scary truth is that, although we may be more media-savvy and cynical than our parents' generation, we are as susceptible as anyone else.

Look at how Skodas have changed the way they are perceived. From the butt of a hundred jokes about their poor quality a few years ago, today Skoda drivers tell each other, 'they're basically VWs', and nod knowingly at one another.

Was Angus Deayton any less funny or adept at delivering a line after his exposé in the *News of the World* than before it? He was the same man. All that had changed was our perception of him.

Look at the way in which fear of crime increases when a gory murder or savage beating is plastered across the newspapers. Actual crime figures may be falling, but the media makes us believe that we are more likely to be victims.

The fact is that our version of 'the truth' is dependent on a range of factors. We all view the world around us through different eyes. We all assess information differently based on our own experiences, perspectives and prejudices. In communications, there is a gap between the facts and a person's understanding of them, and this gap is where the spin doctor operates.

Key points

- Spin doctoring is about presenting your message in the best possible light – not lying, cheating or dissembling.
- Everyone is at it – even journalists.
- There is no such thing as 'the truth'; only our own versions of it.
- Perceptions often matter more than realities.
- The medium can be the message.

Chapter Two
Why Bother?

A good reputation is more valuable than money.
Publius Syrus (1ˢᵗ century BC)

Why should anyone bother? Hasn't all this obsession with style, spin and packaging gone too far? If the product you sell is good, or the message you say is truthful, surely people will accept you at face value?

Wrong.

Your reputation matters

Whoever you are, your reputation matters. What people say about you, what they think, how you are valued and judged, all influence your success or failure in business, in careers, and in life. Reputations matter for organisations, places and people.

In the corporate world, reputation is increasingly seen as being as important an asset as capital or buildings. For many global firms which could, if they chose, open or close factories anywhere on the face of the planet, or sack thousands and survive, reputation is *the* most important asset, even more than people. People can be hired, sacked, or retrained. A reputation is as delicate as an orchid and as fragile as a china vase. It can take decades to build a good one, and minutes to destroy it. One stupid slip and it's in pieces all over the floor.

A good reputation creates goodwill between an organisation and its important audiences. With goodwill on your side, you can achieve most things. Without it, people will show an alarming resistance to doing the things you want them to do. Goodwill can be created through a thousand and one encounters over time. Good service in a shop or restaurant, prompt delivery by a home shopping company, intelligent and targeted marketing, a friendly word and a remembered name: these are the things which generate goodwill between commercial organisations and their customers.

Without a good reputation, organisations and individuals cannot function properly.

How to get a good reputation

The best metaphor to describe how to get a good reputation is to imagine a building. It needs firm foundations and solid pillars to hold it up. All the ornate decoration, carvings and paint in the world will not support a building built on shaky foundations or with crumbling cement.

Marks & Spencer has built up a solid reputation over decades by selling us quality clothing and yummy food. It has a reputation for being a good employer. It is famous for its no-questions-asked returns policy. No one is going to die in a ditch for Marks & Spencer, but it does occupy a small piece of the British cultural landscape and enjoys a high level of sympathy from the public. So when it started to have financial problems, most people gave it the benefit of the doubt because it had reputational 'credit in the bank.' Most people want to see Marks & Spencer survive in the high street. Compare M&S to C&A. Where are C&A today? Long gone from the high street, and not much missed. In part, this is because C&A never generated the same kind of reservoir of goodwill that M&S had, and no one really cared whether they survived or not.

So a good reputation can help you survive a crisis because, in a 50:50 situation, people give you the benefit of the doubt. A good reputation is constructed by doing one or two things well.

In the case of Marks & Spencer it was sandwiches and underwear. Once it diversified into luggage, financial products and ball gowns, things started to go wrong. You need to decide what you want to be known for doing well.

What's true of organisations is also true of places. Cities and countries have reputations which have many of the same characteristics as people and companies. Consider the following statements: 'I'm taking a mini-break in Glasgow', 'We're going to New York for the weekend' or 'we've bought a flat in the middle of Manchester'. In the early 21st century these conversational gambits would be met with a positive response – everyone knows Glasgow is filled with galleries, theatres, restaurants and bars, that Manchester's city centre is a lively cosmopolitan place, and that New York is the place to get a great exchange rate and fantastic shopping and where everyone looks like Jennifer Aniston and Matt LeBlanc. But what if you'd heard those statements in the 1970s? Buy a flat in Manchester's centre? You must be mad – everyone else is moving to the suburbs. Glasgow? It's full of drunks. And as for New York? Crime, drugs, gangs, murder, and the *Kids from Fame*. Best stay at home. The reputation of these places has transformed in under 30 years.

Partly it was because of changes in the local economies, regeneration schemes, and the cultural rebirth of these cities. But it was also because of lively and imaginative 'place marketing' campaigns. To exclaim 'I ♥ NY' was a bold statement in the seventies and eighties. Very few people did love New York. Yet today the statement, which appears on a million T-shirts and baseball hats, is part of mainstream pop culture. Glasgow ran its 'Glasgow's Miles Better' campaign between 1983 and 1989, aimed at opinion-formers and professionals ('ABC1s' in the advertising jargon). The image of the city rapidly changed thanks to the campaign, and high-profile successes such as becoming City of Culture. Manchester too has worked hard to improve its image. When I lived there in the

1980s, the city centre emptied after work, and most of the canal-side buildings were empty. Today the city is filled with new bars and restaurants, loft-style flats, and new galleries and museums.

In London, the reputation of places changes year by year. Islington used to known for slums and crime. Now it is famous for sun-dried tomatoes and focaccia. The gritty drama *Up the Junction* was filmed in the 1960s around Clapham Junction's tenements, rough pubs and factories. By the 1990s, the yuppies had taken over. Even as late as the early 1980s, *Minder* depicted a working-class Fulham which has long gone, pushed aside by people moving down from Chelsea. Today, London neighbourhoods like Hoxton, Clerkenwell and King's Cross are transforming the way in which they are perceived. The drivers for these changes are often word-of-mouth campaigns amongst estate agents, home buyers, and the property pages of newspapers. A reputation as an up-and-coming area can see property prices soar, and the market-readers create a self-fulfilling prophecy.

So clever marketing and campaigning can change the reputation of a place, just as much as it can a company or product. Most importantly, a good reputation is vital for you. If you are engaged in campaigning, or dealing with the media, or trying to get your cause, message or product some attention, then you cannot succeed if people, and especially journalists, think that you are a waste of space.

Key points

- Good reputations are built over time by doing things that meet or exceed expectations.
- Campaigns can help build reputations.
- Reputations apply to people, places, organisations and products.

How to get a bad reputation

A bad reputation can come over time, through persistent scandal, failure and disappointments (for example, the British royal family or Virgin trains), but far more fun to watch is when it comes from a single cataclysmic event, gaffe or cock-up. Even the most powerful organisations and global brands can be laid low by arrogance, poor planning and media gaffes. A major public relations disaster can have different effects on your reputation, based on the extent of the damage, the circumstances, the current state of public morals, and the mood of a handful of journalists that morning.

The battle for reputation is an asymmetric form of warfare. Huge corporations can be damaged by a handful of activists armed with websites and mobile phones. A massive marketing budget can count for nothing against a stupid gaffe and an unforgiving media. The McLibel trial, when the McDonald's corporation took a pair of environmental activists to court in a lengthy and costly case, shows the lengths businesses will go to to protect their reputations. The McDonald's case against Helen Steel and David Morris cost £10 million and, at 315 days, was the longest-ever civil trial in English history. It was a classic David and Goliath confrontation, with most people siding with David.

Nearly everyone in the world has heard of Coca Cola. It is a $70 billion global corporation, and its success is anchored in a brown sweet fizzy drink.

When Coca Cola decided to introduce Dasani, a new brand of bottled water into the UK, they cannot possibly, even in the worst nightmares of the best crisis-planning experts in the world, have imagined what a PR disaster was about to befall them. And why would they? Dasani is the US's second best-selling bottled water. They allocated £7 million to the launch. They invested in a 'NASA-approved reverse osmosis multi-barrier filtration system'. What could possibly go wrong? What went wrong was that an enterprising journalist on a trade magazine noticed that, unlike most spring waters sold in the UK, Dasani was tap water which had undergone a filtration process in a plant in Sidcup.

So Dasani cost 95p per 500ml bottle; the same amount of tap water would cost 0.03p. When the newspapers got hold of it, they pointed out a remarkably similar story-line in the popular BBC television comedy *Only Fools and Horses*, when Del Boy and Rodney bottled 'Peckham Spring' from the mains. Even this PR disaster was just about survivable. But when illegal levels of cancer-causing bromates were discovered in the product, the game was up. The launch was cancelled, the product withdrawn. More significant than the £25 million loss for the company was the damage to its reputation. What are the lessons? People don't like being taken for mugs. You can't ignore local cultural factors like the *Only Fools...* resonance. Even the biggest and best in the world, like Coca Cola, can be humbled by the media.

Sometimes PR disasters are unpredictable. Paddy Ashdown, leader of the Liberal Democrats, had an affair with his secretary and the papers found out. Far from being damaged by the revelations, his personal ratings went up, largely because of the honest and straightforward way in which he dealt with the issue. The Ashdown-level disaster serves to enhance your reputation by making you seem more interesting. When John Prescott struck an egg-throwing fox-hunting-supporter in the face, it did little to damage his reputation. In some quarters, it improved it. So what on paper should be a career-ending gaffe may actually work in the opposite direction.

At the other end of the scale is the Ratner-level disaster, when a chance remark can cause meltdown. Gerald Ratner, a successful high-street jeweller, made a speech at an Institute of Directors event in 1991. In front of his peers, he said that his business success was built on selling 'crap'. His audience probably chortled. But when the remark was reported in the newspapers, his customers were outraged. His sales dropped. He lost the business. It took ten years to build his chain of jewellers, and ten seconds to throw it down the toilet.

The case of Gerald Ratner is distinctly different from other calamitous business failures such as the fall of Barings Bank. Barings went out of business because of huge losses resulting from abysmal internal checks and balances and the greed and foolishness of Nick Leeson. Barings fell because of actual financial weaknesses, followed by a collapse in public confidence. But Ratners fell purely because of a swift collapse of reputation. The shops, staff, products and prices were the same after Gerald Ratner's remarks to the IoD as before it. According to every traditional method of accounting or business analysis, Ratners was worth the same after his gaffe as before it. What had changed was that Ratner's reputation was transformed and trust had evaporated. The impact of an intangible factor – reputation – had a very tangible effect on the business's chances of survival.

Ratner is a major example of a gaffe. The gaffe is a verbal or symbolic mistake which damages your reputation because of what it says about you. Often a gaffe is a statement or use of language which may be acceptable to one group of people, but is insulting to another.

A few stupid remarks can speak volumes about a company's view of its customers. How about this story from the BBC, reported in March 2003?

Anger over 'pikey' slur

People who shop at Sainsbury's in Hereford have been described as 'pikeys' by a senior manager at the supermarket.

Lisa Collins, who is in charge of the company's health and beauty section, made the comments while addressing a recent conference.

She told her audience that Sainsbury's had tried new in-store health and beauty departments in two 'comfortable' areas of the country – Solihull, West Midlands, and Leamington Spa, Warwickshire.

Ms Collins said the company was to use the idea in other UK stores, including the one in Hereford, adding: 'Or, as we call them, our pikey customers.'

Or this from the BBC in July 2001:

Topman customers 'hooligans'

Fashion bosses are battling to avoid a public relations disaster after the marketing chief of the Topman chain said its customers were 'hooligans'.

In an interview with a trade magazine, David Shepherd said Topman customers only wore a suit for their first interview or their first court appearance.

These gaffes reveal an attitude towards customers which does not display much respect or gratitude.

A gaffe can tell you what a company thinks about its own products. Here's another BBC story from October 2003 about a senior figure from Barclays:

Barclay chief's gaffe recalls Ratner howler

They call it 'doing a Ratner' – in memory of the famous gaffe committed by Gerald Ratner back in 1991, when he admitted selling 'crap' in his High Street shops.

Now the boss of the UK's largest credit card company has done it in such a spectacular fashion that it left business observers open-mouthed.

Barclays chief executive Matt Barrett candidly criticised his own product, suggesting that the astute consumer would do well to steer well clear of it.

Giving evidence to the Commons' Treasury select committee he said he did not use credit cards from his own subsidiary, Barclaycard, because it was simply too expensive.

He also revealed that he advised his four offspring to have nothing to do with credit cards either.

'I do not borrow on credit cards. I have four young children. I give them advice not to pile up debts on their credit cards.'

Matt Barrett's financial advice to his children is perfectly sound, but it seems hypocritical coming from the man responsible for issuing millions of credit cards to other people's children.

A reputation is your reservoir of goodwill – it can be filled a few drops at a time, and let out in a mighty torrent if the dam bursts. Once it's gone, all you're left with is fish gulping for air, weeds, and wet feet. If you don't take steps to manage your reputation, to protect it, to enhance it and to promote its positive aspects, you run the risk of your message being lost and your good deeds going unnoticed. Forget people, buildings, even cash in the bank. Without a good reputation, you are nothing.

Key points
- A negative reputation can be created by a single slip-up or gaffe.
- The media can destroy your reputation.
- A spokesperson for your organisation holds your reputation in their hands.
- Gaffes can be avoided by thinking about how different audiences will react.

The role of the media
To what extent does the media mould opinion and affect reputation? We like to dismiss the power of the newspapers, radio and television, but their influence is profound. Articles in newspapers

and programmes on radio and television do more than bring us news and entertain us. They introduce us to new ideas, words, cultures and people. They introduce new words into our thoughts and conversations. Who knew what a 'tsunami' was before December 2004? The media introduces us to concepts we didn't know were important: al-Qaeda, MRSA, skunk, chavs or hoodies. The role of the media in shaping popular culture is deeper than simply bringing new ideas to our attention. The media also moulds the way in which we perceive things.

Journalist John Lloyd, in his book *What the Media are Doing to our Politics*, writes:

> The media, in the 21st century, are in Britain at the height of their powers – a position shared by their counterparts in no other country, not even the US. The population watches, on average, 28 hours of television a week, and listens to 24 hours of radio a week; in 2003, nearly 35 million people read a daily or Sunday newspaper and nearly 25 million people accessed the internet.

Lloyd continues:

> Nothing – not religious belief, not political debate and argument, not even conversation with friends and family – possesses the command over mass attention that the media have taken as their own. Their themes dominate public and private lives. Their definitions of what is right or wrong, true or false, impose themselves on politics and on the public domain. Their narratives construct the world we don't immediately experience – which for nearly all of us, is most of the world.

Reputations are made and broken by the media. When Ratner said his jewellery was crap, only a few dozen heard his remarks live. Millions more read about them in the tabloids. It was the reporting of the gaffe, not the gaffe itself, which led to his spectacular fall. When Prince Harry wore a swastika armband to a party, it was the media coverage (and especially the front page of *The Sun*) which damaged his already tarnished reputation. Even Jo Moore's email only became a career-ending problem when a disgruntled civil servant leaked it to the press weeks later.

It is impossible to overestimate the importance of the media in shaping the reputations of companies, organisations, places, products, political parties and famous people. That is why they all spend so much time, money and effort trying to influence what the media says about them.

Key points

- Your reputation is your greatest asset.
- You need to protect it, not leave it to chance.
- The media influences how you are perceived.
- Beyond an immediate circle of friends, colleagues and neighbours, the media can help you build a positive image.
- The media can destroy a reputation in seconds.

Chapter Three
Understanding the Media

Basically you're all overpaid and we hate you.
                DTI press officer's unguarded comment to journalists

Spin doctors must understand the media and the people who work in it. To be a successful spin doctor you must know what gets journalists' juices flowing, and conversely what makes them want to slam the phone down. You have to be able, in the words of Harper Lee, to stand in their shoes and walk around.

That's why former journalists can make effective spin doctors: because they understand the structure and culture of the modern media. The most important attribute for the spin doctor is to understand journalists and the organisations they work for: what motivates them, what excites them, what annoys them and the pressures of the job from which they suffer. It is also vital to understand the news-gathering process and the structure and machinery of the modern media. You have to be able to talk the same language.

Most journalists are hard-working, committed and intelligent. Journalists tend to have a sense of professionalism and pride in their job, which they see as an essential part of the democratic process. 'Freedom of the press' as the mark of a free society is a concept they take seriously. Their belief in seeking out the truth is mostly sincere. When a journalist such as the *New York Times*'s Jayson Blair is caught out making up sources, quotes, interviews, and even whole events, then we are rightly shocked.

Most journalists have undergone specialist training. In the UK, journalism training is governed by the National Council for the Training of Journalists (NCTJ). The NCTJ accredits journalism qualifications in colleges and universities and maintains standards. A NCTJ qualification is a prerequisite for most jobs in journalism (with the exception of columnists, who require only a lively and controversial take on life.)

Many journalists have survived at the lower reaches of the profession on abysmal pay and conditions. The *Guardian Media Guide* describes the paths into the job as 'many and vague, usually mundane, and always badly paid'. Journalism is a trade where 'paying your dues' counts.

The structure of the media

The first step is to understand what kind of journalist you need to talk to, in which type of media. The job title 'journalist' covers a multitude of sins, from the trainee (or 'cub') reporter on a local newspaper to highly paid and famous columnists on national newspapers such as Simon Jenkins, Richard Littlejohn, Polly Toynbee, Simon Heffer, Alison Pearson, Roy Hattersley or Julie Burchill. 'Journalist' also includes radio reporters, television researchers, freelancers and those working on trade and technical magazines.

Each of these different types of journalist has a widely different agenda, requirements, pressures and specialism. Different types of media have different types of audiences, and your message will be differently understood if it appears on GMTV, or the Jeremy Vine show on Radio Two, compared to the *Financial Times* or *The Economist*.

The media can be divided into three parts: print, broadcast and online.

Print
International newspapers
National newspapers
Regional newspapers

Local newspapers
Trade and technical magazines
Ethnic and faith-based newspapers and magazines
In-house magazines
Community publications
Club and society publications

Broadcast
National television
Local television
National radio
Local radio
Community radio

Online
Internet versions of national and local newspapers and magazines
Internet-only news sites
Blogs (weblogs by individuals or collectives)

Many of the methods of news-gathering and production are similar across different media, and at the higher reaches journalists work in both print and broadcast at the same time, or skip between the two camps. Radio interviewers appear on television, television presenters write columns and books, and print journalists give interviews on the radio. For example, Andrew Marr was the BBC's chief political correspondent, has written a column for the *Daily Telegraph*, was editor of *The Independent*, and now has taken over from David Frost on BBC1's Sunday morning current affairs slot. Piers Morgan worked on *The Sun*, was editor of the *Mirror*, and now appears on TV. At the higher reaches of journalism there is a great deal of crossover between different types of media.

Newspapers

National newspapers
When we talk of the 'press', national newspapers are what most people think of. The national newspapers carry huge authority and influence, and carry the best, and worst, of British journalism. Fifty-five per cent of the British public aged over 15 reads a national newspaper on an average weekday. This figure has fallen from almost 80 per cent 25 years ago, and the newspaper market has become increasingly bitterly contested – with the circulation war having a profound effect on newspaper design, content and standards of journalism.

There are ten national daily newspapers. They can be divided into 'pops', 'red tops' or tabloids ('tabs'): *The Sun, Daily Mirror, Daily Star*; mid-markets: *Daily Express, Daily Mail*; and the broadsheets and compacts: *The Guardian, The Times, Financial Times, Daily Telegraph, The Independent* (both *The Times* and *The Independent* are now available only in a compact size).

Added to these are the national Sunday newspapers: *News of the World, Sunday Mirror, Mail on Sunday, The People, Sunday Times, Sunday Express, Sunday Telegraph, The Observer* and *Independent on Sunday*. Two other titles are national and appear in newspaper format – the *Morning Star* (the Communist daily) and the *Daily Sport* (an adult comic). Also the London *Evening Standard* has a huge readership and enormous influence, can be bought in most UK cities, but is technically a regional paper.

There has been a trend towards concentration of ownership. The national newspaper business is controlled by 11 owners: Associated Newspapers (*Daily Mail* and *Mail on Sunday*), Express Newspapers, *Financial Times,* Guardian Media Group, Independent News and Media UK Limited, News International (Rupert Murdoch's lot – *The Times, Sunday Times, The Sun, News of the World*), Scotsman Publications, Scottish Daily Record &

Sunday Mail, Sport Newspapers, Telegraph Group Limited (controlled by the Barclay brothers), and Trinity Mirror.

Readerships vary greatly between these newspapers. *The Sun* sells over 3.1 million copies, and is read by around ten million people every day. The *Financial Times* sells around 425,000 copies. Yet for the spin doctor, it is not just a numbers game. More important than the raw circulation figures is an understanding of which social class and profession tends to read what.

Also, newspapers have their own political slant: the *Mirror* is Labour, the *Daily Telegraph* is Tory. *The Guardian* and *Daily Mail* are no fans of the Labour government, but for entirely different reasons. A financial spin doctor will target the *FT* because of the kind of people that read it (business leaders, investors etc.), rather than the volume. Political spin doctors recognise the value of mass circulation tabloids like *The Sun* for spreading a political message to millions. When they want to communicate subtler messages to their own parties, they might chose newspapers which are read by party members. An article placed in *The Guardian* will reach most of the Labour membership, despite that newspaper's hostility to the party. Similarly, whenever the Tories have something to say to Tories, they tend to choose the *Daily Telegraph*.

Local papers

Local newspapers are more important than you might think. There are over 100 daily local and regional newspapers and 1,300 weeklies in the UK. Even the freesheet shoved through your letterbox gets audiences in tens of thousands. Freesheets can even reach audiences in the hundreds of thousands (*Manchester Metro News*: 300,000; *Nottingham Post*: 150,000; *Teesside Herald and Post: 160,000*).

If you're one of those people who complains that 'they're all adverts' then you should be asking why so many advertisers pay hard cash to place ads. It's not for love. It's because local papers are read by enough people to make advertising worthwhile. Local weekly and daily newspapers attract over £2 billion of advertising revenue per year (only television attracts more) and over 80 per cent of adults read their local paper. Forty per cent of adults claim to prefer their local paper to the nationals.

These papers can have huge readerships. The London *Evening Standard* is bought by over 370,000 people every day in the Greater London area (more than the number who buy *The Independent* in the whole of the UK.)

The *Birmingham Evening Mail* has a circulation of over 100,000 people, as does the *Manchester Evening News*. That's a lot of people.

So let us hear no more about them being unimportant or not mattering. If a mention in the *Liverpool Echo* can reach 135,000 people in a single day, the locals and regionals matter to the spin doctor.

Often the smaller titles, such as the *Yellow Advertiser* in South Essex, are staffed by just one or two news journalists, making them great targets. The journalists tend to be young, first- or second-job-bers, and keen to make their mark. Most stay on the paper for only a year or two, and most dream of a job on a national newspaper.

If your targeting is right, your story has a strong local angle, and your news release is well-written, you have a good chance of success. Sometimes your words will appear verbatim. I once sent a news release to a freesheet which not only printed the text word for word, but also the news release instructions to the subs, including 'ends' and 'for more information contact Paul Richards …'

The local angle is the key, though. If the story is about an event in the wrong part of town or wrong village (off 'the patch'), the journalist won't touch it. Gareth Weekes, former editor of the *Salisbury Journal,* put it well: 'world-shattering events could be happening in Devizes … but not a line would appear in the *Salisbury Journal* because our world ends at the village of Upavon'.

Local papers want a steady diet of local stories about local people, events, or places. Local campaigns and pressure groups can do well; or local interest groups like the local history society, local hospital league of friends, or local teams and clubs.

My first job on the *Buckinghamshire Advertiser* was to go through the 'deaths' announcements in the national newspapers, spot any local people who had died, and phone their grieving families to see if there was a story. I was 16 at the time, and understandably balked at this ghoulish task, but the editor made me do it anyway. 'If you can't do this,' he said, 'forget being a journalist.' So I went off to university instead.

The way local journalists carry out this unpleasant task, incidentally, is to phone the next of kin and claim that they are writing a special tribute to the deceased ('a respected and loved local figure'). What they are really after is to discover if the deceased was found wearing women's underwear with a bag on their head and an orange stuffed in their mouth.

Magazines

There has been an explosion of titles in the magazine sector in the last 20 years. In the last decade the number of magazines produced has increased by a third, and circulation has increased by over 10 per cent. Magazines are now available for every leisure and lifestyle interest, from women's mags like *Cosmopolitan, Elle, Prima, She* or *Woman's Own* to consumer titles like *Good Housekeeping, BBC Good Food Magazine, Radio Times, Total InterNet* and *Family Circle*, and 'new lad' magazines like *Loaded* and *FHM*. There are also current affairs and political magazines which reach important audiences, like *New Statesman, Spectator*, and *The Economist*. The top-selling magazines have readerships in the millions (*Sky TV Guide*: 6,600,000; *Take a Break*: 1,200,000; *Radio Times*: 1,100,000).

The news content of these magazines is minimal, and the lead-times for publication may be months. The approach you take is very different from contacting a news room. Magazines use free-lancers for much of their material, and so the relationship you need to develop with the journalist is harder to pin down. If you want to place stories and features in magazines, you need to plan months in advance and place material which suits the style and content of the target title. An article on homelessness might make it into *New Statesman*, but won't even get read at *Maxim*. A story about a group of women mountaineers climbing Mount Everest would be of interest to *Cosmopolitan*, but not to *Loaded* (unless they were climbing it naked). Magazines want human interest, not hard news.

The benefit of having your message appear in these lifestyle and consumer magazines is that people tend to be less cynical and scep-tical about what they read in magazines. A serious message which appears in a consumer mag has greater impact. Political parties have begun to target these titles, especially women's magazines, because they can reach audiences in ways which the traditional news media have exhausted. During the 1992 general election the Labour Party produced a mock women's magazine filled with frothy stories and big pictures which activists were supposed to go about the country leaving in hairdressers' and dentists' waiting rooms. The sexy hunk on the cover, in jeans and open-neck shirt, was a rising star called Tony Blair.

Trade and technicals

These tend to appear as the 'joke' title in the missing words round of *Have I Got News for You*, but for many thousands of journalists, publications like *British Baker* and *Dairy Farmer* are their bread and butter.

Amateur Gardening, Angling Times, Bee World, Bird Watching, The Budgerigar, Flying Saucer Review, Freemasonry Today, The Grocer, Helicopter International, Local Historian, Manchester United Magazine, Materials Reclamation Weekly, Municipal Journal, Office

Equipment News, Packaging Week, Pig Farming, Rugby World, Shoe and Leather News, Sporting Gun, Structural Engineer, Timber Trades Journal, Water Bulletin, Which Motorcaravan, Your Cat and *Zionist Review* are magazines which delight, amuse and make the day of millions of people. These titles are also eagerly awaited by thousands of people in the relevant business or trade, as a source of unique information and news. You may prefer watching concrete dry to reading *Concrete Quarterly*, but for some people it's the highlight of their week.

They can be the source of news stories for the nationals and broadcasters. A medical story might break in the *Lancet*, a political story in the *Spectator*, or a science story in *New Scientist*.

Broadcast

Television
In terms of mass communication, television is the most powerful medium – that's why advertisers spend millions to promote their products on television. Spin doctors take TV very seriously indeed because of this potency. Ninety-nine per cent of UK households have a TV set, 64 per cent have two and 28 per cent have three or more. Forty per cent of leisure time is spent watching TV. A visual image is far more powerful than the printed word.

In Britain the TV sector breaks down like this: the public sector (the BBC) which is funded via the TV licence fee and broadcast nationally; the private sector (ITV), funded by advertising revenue and broadcast regionally on 16 local stations and nationally on Channel Four and Channel Five; and satellite and cable, which is funded by adverts and subscriptions.

In our times, television has undergone a revolution. From the days when TV meant a choice of three channels, today people can access hundreds. Since the 1980s we have seen the launch of Channel Four, Channel Five, breakfast TV, the introduction of cable and satellite, and the BBC's 24-hour news programme.

The proliferation of channels has not meant a proliferation of news reporting on television, but there are opportunities for spin doctors. Stations like Sky News, BBC News 24, and cable channels have a great deal of airtime to fill. They have an insatiable appetite for talking heads, and can be targeted for interviews and comment.

Television news programmes remain the best target for spin doctors: the daily bulletins are monitored closely by the political parties, and producers are phoned if they sense any bias or omissions. The most important are the 6.30pm ITN news and the 6.00pm BBC news bulletins, and then the 10.00pm BBC and 10.30pm ITN bulletins. These news programmes are known in the business by the times they start. You should refer to 'the Ten' or the 'the Six' if you want to sound like you know what you're talking about. You can occasionally spot the spin by following the progress of a particular story on these bulletins during a day. The coverage may change from lunch-time to teatime to evening as the story develops, new interviews are edited in, new angles appear, and the spin doctors have gone to work. The local television stations have local news operations which can be targeted with good local stories with plenty of visual interest.

Programmes such as *Newsnight* and *World in Action* maintain high standards of journalism on terrestrial TV, and remain the most difficult programmes to influence, as competition is fierce. Other programmes like *Trisha* have studio audiences which are easy to get people into, especially if you have something interesting or controversial to say. In the past, people have been exposed masquerading as 'serial guests' on these programmes, wearing disguises and pretending to be reformed criminals, drug addicts, or whatever.

The next big change to hit television is the move to digital broadcasting, which is already starting to replace analogue. There are fears that digital broadcasting will increase the costs of viewing, and exclude some people from the plethora of channels and services which the new technology will allow. What it will mean is that television will become more interactive, be used for home shopping and banking, and cease to be a medium which chooses what you watch and when. Instead, television programmes and films will become available on demand, thus wiping out the video and DVD industry.

Radio

Like television, the radio industry is split between the BBC and the commercial sector, and organised on a national and local level.

The BBC has prestige programmes like *Today* and *World at One*, which set the news agenda and reach important opinion-forming audiences.

The country is covered in local radio stations. Each major town has a BBC station and one or more commercial stations; York, for example has BBC Radio York and Minster FM; Manchester has GMR (the BBC) and Key 103.

Although the figure dipped slightly in the latter half of the 1990s, 85 per cent of over-15s listen to the radio at least once a week. All radio stations carry an element of news. The BBC has its major international news operation, using reporters in common with television as part of its 'bi-media' approach. The 40 BBC local radio stations use news fed from the national operation, and from their own newsdesks. They are supplied material from the GNS (the General News Service), which makes live interviews available to a range of local stations one after the other from a single studio. Commercial radio uses its own reporters and Independent Radio News (IRN), based at the ITN headquarters. Stations like Talk Radio, Radio Five Live, and London's News Direct rely on a constant supply of interviewees. Local radio needs local stories on the same criteria as local papers – with the obvious difference that radio needs people to talk about the story.

The smaller stations have very few staff, especially at the weekends, and so it is important to make the right approach. There is a world of difference between phoning at five minutes to the hour, when the news presenter is desperately finishing off scripts for the hourly news bulletin, and five minutes after the hour when the bulletin is over and the presenter has time to talk to you. Radio newsrooms have separate phone numbers from the main switchboard numbers, so if you need to phone them over a weekend or after hours, you need the right number.

Online

Most news available is also available on the internet. All of the national newspapers have websites, most of which are free to view. The *Daily Telegraph*'s website – www.telegraph.co.uk – allows free viewing of all the news up to one week old; archives are available through a paid-for subscription service. The *Financial Times*' website – www.ft.com – allows a search of the *FT*'s news as well as news on other sites around the world. This is predominately a free service, though a subscription allows access to other tools and searches. *The Guardian* website – www.guardian.co.uk – is free and access to the archives is also free, but a subscription service provides a pdf version of the newspaper in the same format as the print version. This service offers no extra contents, only a format which is, for some, more easy to navigate. *The Times* website – www.times-online.co.uk – has a subscription service for the older archives but most of the news is free to view. *The Independent* website – www.independent.co.uk – is only available on subscription.

The major TV news channels have websites on which the news programmes have continuously updated pages. For example, BBC news has an online version which is updated 24 hours a day. The major BBC news programmes also have their own pages. The BBC radio stations have their own website pages – www.bbc.co.uk/radio – on which you can listen to the programmes live or up to a week after airing. The same is true for all the major television and radio networks.

The benefits to a spin doctor of news online are threefold. First, online news sites have almost unlimited space (hence the name of *The Guardian*'s site is *Guardian Unlimited*) so they can use more articles than the print version and longer versions of the articles. This means that you have a better chance of getting your piece in.

The second benefit is that the articles can be viewed by people around the world whenever they choose. Most of these articles will remain on the online archives for years and a simple search will bring them up whereas a print paper will have long ago been sent to the recyclers.

Third, the online news sites are continuously updated and are, therefore, always looking for comments and articles on breaking news stories. If they know that you are able to produce a quote on major news stories quickly, they will keep coming back to you in the future.

However, there are downsides to online news. For example, there is less prestige attached to having a piece in the online version of a national newspaper as opposed to the print version. Also, if your article doesn't have links on the main pages, it will be difficult for people to come across it accidentally as websites are huge and can be difficult to navigate. The best way to avoid this problem is to have an article which has links on as many of the website's main pages as possible.

The main page of an online newspaper is the website's homepage – the first page you get when you type in the basic web address. However, each section will have its own front page as well.

For example, *Times Online* has a front page at www.timeson-line.co.uk and then the health section has its own front page at www.timesonline.co.uk/section/0,,589,00.html. The best way to make sure that your piece is seen by the maximum number of people is to have a link to it on the site's main page and one or more of the sub-sections' main pages.

For example, an article about a high profile politician might feature on the Guardian Unlimited front page. As a story about politics it might also have a link on the Guardian Unlimited politics front page. If that story is also relevant to the society pages, it could also have a link on that front page. Anybody visiting any of those three main pages would be able to see the link and access that article without searching for it.

It is important to remember that the staff on the online version are usually different from the staff of the print version; it is usually best to contact them separately. Even if your story appears in the print version, most of which will be replicated online, it is worth remembering that the website has more space and may be interested in expanding upon a story.

Blogs

Blogs are self-published diaries or running commentaries, often covering specialist areas. Some have a comment section for readers to post up their thoughts. The Baghdad Blogger came to fame for publishing his online diary during the Iraq War. Belle de Jour was a blog published by a London call girl. Many journalists – for example Stephen Pollard, Johann Hari and Melanie Phillips – publish blogs which contain both new material and versions of articles published in magazines and newspapers. The problem with blogs is that they are usually not written by professional journalists, and can descend into ranting and raving. Also they attract weird people on to their comment sections, which become the online equivalent of the graffiti on a toilet wall. Some people get quite obsessive, rude, or disturbed. Spin doctors should keep an eye on the blogs which are relevant to their sector, because often it is in cyberspace that malicious rumours or lies can be spread, and find their way into the mainstream media. For now, though, blogs have small readerships and are mostly irrelevant.

News agencies

A news agency is a news-gathering organisation which sells its news and information to the print and broadcast media. National and international agencies such as the Press Association (PA), Associated Press, Bloomberg Business News or Reuters serve newsrooms and other organisations via an online link-up, still known as a 'wire'. 'What's running on the wires?' means what stories are appearing from the news agencies? Smaller agencies might specialise in particular subject areas, or concentrate on a specific geographical area (e.g. Bournemouth News and Print Services, Anglia Press Agency).

The Press Association (PA), jointly owned by the national newspapers, is the main news agency in the UK. It has a vital role in the creation of news, and is therefore of great importance in the world of spin doctoring. The Press Association is not a media outlet in its own right – it supplies news stories and information via online computers.

PA has staff reporters, specialist correspondents, photographers, feature writers and editors, in the same way as a national newspaper. It also has a radio service.

News stories appear on the screen under 'slugs' or short headings, with the time they were written or the embargo on their use, and are supplied direct to newsrooms, businesses, and Parliament. Even some posh London clubs have PA (still supplied via a telex on to sheets of paper which are pinned up on a board). Subscribers to PA can then use the material in their own publications – either wholesale, or as the basis for their own reporting of the story. PA also supplies photos online, diary dates, and quotes.

I was the lowly Labour Party press office apparatchik assigned to Tony Blair for a day in summer 1993 when the great man was Shadow Home Secretary. We caught wind of a breaking news story about a prisoner dying in the back of a van whilst in the custody of the private firm Group 4. Tony Blair's second thought (after sympathy) was to get a quote ('the Group 4 farce has turned to tragedy') on the PA wire as soon as possible, because of the importance of PA in shaping a breaking news story. Within minutes Blair's line was running on radio and TV.

If you have something worth saying, you can usually bypass the PA reporters and get straight through to 'copy-takers' who will input your quote or statement immediately (just ask for 'copy'). PA also receives a blizzard of news releases on a minute-by-minute basis, and has a healthy disregard for most of them.

If a story, quote or event appears on PA, it appears in the newsrooms of virtually every important media outlet in the country. A single phone call to PA can lead to coverage in dozens of newspapers, national and regional, and be picked up for further coverage by the broadcasters.

Different types of journalist

As already mentioned, 'journalist' covers a variety of different functions on newspapers, magazines, radio and television. Let's turn now to the main jobs in the media.

Reporter

At the front line is the reporter, responsible for writing news stories, or delivering reports direct on radio or TV. On a local paper there might be only a handful; on a national newspaper, hundreds. This is the type of journalist most people feel they understand the best: the fearless crusader for truth, the tireless scribe, the exposer of injustice. When people have any kind of direct contact with journalists, it is the reporter they usually face. Reporters have been immortalised in fiction, from Lois Lane and Clark Kent on the *Daily Planet*, to Damien Day, the unscrupulous TV news reporter in *Drop the Dead Donkey*, to the hapless Boot in Evelyn Waugh's *Scoop*.

Specialist correspondent

… is a journalist covering a particular area such as health, sport, personal finance, cooking or defence. They have job titles like 'Health Correspondent' or 'Sports Editor', and are often recognised authorities in their area of expertise. They range from royal reporters such Jennie Bond to political correspondents such as Andrew Marr.

News Editor

This is a more senior position, responsible for allocating stories to reporters, deciding priorities and angles and usually reporting to the editor. This is usually a journalist with a few more years' experience, but who has often been promoted through the ranks of the news reporters.

Sub-editor

This is a specialist function. The sub-editors ('subs') receive the reporters' articles ('copy') via the newspaper's computer system, and 'weave their magic' (if you believe the subs) or 'hack it to pieces' (if you believe the reporters). The subs' job is to check the spelling, grammar, style and length of the piece, all of which they might change. They also write captions for photographs, 'panels' (the sections of text pulled out of an article and placed between two lines, used to break up long articles) and 'standfirsts' (the text between the headline and the main text, often used on features and longer news pieces.) The subs also lay out the page.

Subbing might be extremely heavy, in the case of a tabloid newspaper where space is at a premium, or lighter on a weekly title. They might phone the reporter for clarification, or refer the article to the lawyers for legal checking. As reporters develop their skills on a particular newspaper, the need for subbing becomes less, as they automatically write to suit the newspaper's own house style.

Subs are also the heroes of the headline. On the tabloids, where bold, attention-grabbing headlines are the most important part of the paper, the subs' craft can be best seen, with a daily dose of puns, alliteration and short, sharp words. Famous headlines such as 'Gotcha' or 'Freddy Starr Ate My Hamster' are the work of subs.

Editor

On a newspaper the editor is the boss with whom the buck stops. They will be a journalist of many years' standing, and will aim to influence the overall style, content and tone of the paper. Usually the editor will report direct to the owner of the newspaper. On the nationals, the editor can become a famous figure in their own right, such as Kelvin MacKenzie, Andrew Neil, Piers Morgan or Andreas Whittam Smith. The hiring and firing of editors can become news in itself – for example, when Piers Morgan was ousted from his position at the *Mirror* in 2004 for publishing what he thought were photographs of British soldiers torturing Iraqi prisoners. The photographs were forgeries. Morgan's defence was that the stories 'illustrated the reality' even if the actual photos were taken several thousand miles from Iraq.

In TV and radio, the editor is in overall charge of a particular programme or series. They are responsible for the general tone and content, and take the rap if something goes wrong or provokes complaints.

Section Editor

On a newspaper, different parts of the paper will have separate editors: for example, the business pages editor, the women's pages editor, or the colour supplement editor.

Producer

In radio and TV, the producer is responsible for the technical production of a programme or section of a programme (a 'package'). There is a move in TV towards multi-skilled producer/reporters who produce the segment of a programme, and also provide the on-screen comment and 'sign-off' at the end.

Assistant Producer (AP)

In radio and TV, this is a more junior version of the producer, working to a producer, and often learning on the job. This role should not be confused with *Production Assistant (PA)* which is the person (usually young and female) responsible for the administrative side of programme-making, such as booking cars for guests, sorting out locations and expenses and ordering the sandwiches.

Researcher

These are the people in TV – usually young and thrusting – who provide the ideas, planning and research for programmes. These are the people who will read news releases, monitor the newspapers and rival stations, spot trends and come up with imaginative ideas. They tend to be starting out in the business, and want to be promoted to APs or reporters.

Freelances

… are journalists who sell their services to different news organisations, but are not directly employed. The National Union of Journalists produces a handy annual directory of freelance journalists, with contact details and favoured subjects. Freelances earn their living by constantly producing enough material to sell to editors. It is a precarious way to make a living, though some of Britain's leading journalists are freelances, including Stephen Pollard, Johann Hari and Michael Crick.

Columnists

… are journalists who write a personal column or page in a newspaper or magazine, setting out their view of current events, what they've been up to that week, which parties they went to, and so on.

Poachers and gamekeepers

Journalists and spin doctors have a healthy disdain for one another. In the early 2000s, this professional rivalry descended at times into outright hostility. Each group believes itself to be superior; yet neither could operate without the other. They are two sides of the same news-creation coin.

Most spin doctors have worked as journalists. Joe Haines and Gerald Kaufman (Harold Wilson's spin doctors) worked on the *Mirror*. Bernard Ingham worked on the *Yorkshire Post*. In 1986 Ingham expressed his empathy with journalists (rather like a cheetah expressing empathy with the gazelle): 'I feel for the reporter … I have shared with him his perishing funerals, his sodden agricultural shows, his grisly murders, his eerie ghost hunts, his endless doorsteps.' Alastair Campbell was a senior political reporter on the *Mirror* and *Today*. Peter Mandelson was a TV producer at London Weekend Television and, for a brief time, a columnist on *The People*. Amanda Platell was on the *Mirror* and *The Independent* before becoming William Hague's spin doctor.

In business too, many former journalists end up as 'Heads of PR' or 'Directors of Communications'. Some set up their own PR firms, such as former Tory spin doctor and *Express* man Charles Lewington, with his firm Media Strategy. Even Max Clifford did a short stint in journalism before becoming press officer for a little-known band from Liverpool called the Beatles. Alastair Campbell's ability to dream up telling phrases that would be echoed in the headlines of the tabloids is legendary. (It was Campbell who put the words 'People's Princess' into the mouth of Tony Blair on the morning after Diana's death – a phrase which became common currency.)

The opportunities may be fewer for spin doctors compared to journalists, but the salaries, conditions and perks tend to be better. It's no surprise that so many of the poachers become gamekeepers.

Key points

- The media comprises many different organisations and individuals.
- Journalists are not all the same.
- Understanding different types of journalist will help you reach the right people in the right way.
- Many spin doctors are former journalists.

Chapter Four
Dealing with Journalists

Enough news is arriving today at any large newspaper office
to make four or five fat novels and fill the news columns
many times over.

Harold Evans

Journalists are individuals with their own foibles, whims, prejudices, and moods. As you work with them, you'll understand their idiosyncrasies. But journalists are also similar in key ways. They have inquiring minds. They ask questions. They don't suffer fools gladly. They process information swiftly, and take snap decisions. They will decide quickly whether or not you are wasting their time.

Journalists want you to be fast, efficient, and above all useful in your dealings with them. They want you to help them do their job better. You can achieve this by giving them stories, secrets, ideas, information, pictures, interviews and quotes. You can fail to do this by trying to persuade them that your dull non-story is the stuff of front pages, that your news release is the most important thing to happen that day, and by failing to understand what the journalist needs and what their deadlines are. Part of the skill of a journalist is being able to sniff out a time-waster on the end of a phone and get rid of them, often brutally, or to spot a source who may be of some use in filling that blank column on page four.

We'll look at the nuts and bolts of dealing with the media later on – the news releases, briefings, photographs and so on. But before we do, there are some basic techniques which put you in the 'useful' category:

Spoon-feeding

The basic job of the spin doctor is to help journalists create news, features, comment and analysis. Journalists do not have the time to interpret complex data or read lengthy reports, and this is a great opportunity to 'help' the journalist in their job by providing handy summaries and guidance.

The popular image of a journalist is that of a news-hound with a note pad in their hand, but the reality is that most journalists are desk-bound, filtering enormous amounts of material that comes to them from the television, radio, newswires, emails and telephones.

Much of modern journalism is as much about filtering, sorting, prioritising and editing as about finding things out.

To succeed in getting noticed and getting printed or broadcast, you must be clear about what you mean, understand what makes a story, have understandable background information, facts, photos and graphics available, and be capable of getting this into the hands of a journalist as soon as possible, by email, fax or motorcycle courier. A charitable view of journalists may be that they spend their time chasing leads, checking sources, and ferreting out the truth, but with a deadline looming and pressure to find a story, none is adverse to a little spoon-feeding from spin doctors.

Speed kills

This means understanding that journalists are working to deadlines, with editors breathing down their necks. If a journalist phones you for some information or a quote, they need answers within minutes, not days. Beating your spin doctoring opponent means being faster than them. The slogan 'speed kills' appeared on the wall of the Clinton War Room during the US presidential elections in 1992. Under the direction of James Carville and George Stephanopoulos (the spin doctors' spin doctors), the Clinton camp had their reaction to events so finely tuned that they could have the

Clinton response and rebuttal to a George Bush senior speech with journalists before Bush even sat down. That meant that time and time again, the news story was not what Bush had said, but what Clinton was saying about what Bush had said.

As a news story develops, especially in the 24-hour world of radio and TV, the angle of the story can be altered by new information on a minute-by-minute basis. The way journalists use interviews during the news cycle changes hour by hour. In a disaster situation the first bulletins feature eye witnesses. Later bulletins feature interviews with the emergency services. Later on, the airline whose plane has crashed, or the country where the earthquake happened, will deploy spokesmen. Last to appear, on BBC2's *Newsnight* and Radio 4's *World Tonight*, will be 'experts' on flight safety, terrorism, earthquakes, hostage psychology or food poisoning, depending on the disaster.

Spin doctors need to understand deadlines. For a huge news story, front pages can be altered, and news bulletins changed at the last minute. Newspapers can change layout from edition to edition on the same day – or even produce special editions to cover a major story such as the death of a Royal. News bulletins can be interrupted during broadcast with a major news story. But this is the exception, not the rule. To influence the news agenda, you have to be ahead of the game, and that means operating well in advance of deadlines. For a daily newspaper, you should aim for late afternoon the previous day, at the very latest. For a Sunday, it should be Friday afternoon. Weekly magazines can take news three to four days in advance of publication, but will have their features worked out weeks in advance. Glossy monthlies like *Cosmopolitan* are designed months in advance.

Timing

When dealing with the media, as with comedy, timing is everything. Because of the relentless regime of deadlines, you have to time your announcements and activities to fit into the journalists' timetables. You also have to time your activities to give yourself maximum advantage. There are times of the year when it's easier to get stories into the newspapers – such as over the summer (the so-called 'silly season'), or between Christmas and New Year. This is because much of national life has shut down, and journalists are looking out for news. Often the journalists on duty are covering for more senior colleagues who are in the South of France or Tuscany, so they may be more open to your approaches. National newspapers come out on a Monday, but often not much happens on a Sunday, so if you offer your story on a 'Sunday for Monday' you might be lucky.

At the higher reaches of spin doctoring, damaging announcements can be timed to minimise their impact. Jo Moore famously sent an email suggesting releasing a government announcement on councillors' allowances on 11 September 2001. She wanted to 'bury' the bad news. She was pilloried by the media when a disgruntled civil servant leaked the email to a newspaper several weeks later, but what had she done wrong? She sent her notorious email after the first plane had crashed into one of the twin towers, but before the full horror of the day's events was clear. In pure spin doctoring terms, her instincts were correct. Only in retrospect does her action look callous. I bet there are plenty of journalists who are glad that no one was recording their initial thoughts and comments that morning.

Is it a coincidence that Downing Street made three announcements simultaneously on Friday 1 October 2004, the day after the end of Labour's annual conference? One concerned Blair's new flash £3.6 million house in Bayswater, the second and third – told directly to Andrew Marr in a television interview – concerned the date of Blair's resignation and the fact that he was going into hospital for a heart operation. You can see the announcements on the retirement date and the new pad as a smokescreen for the news that the PM had heart problems. If the announcement about the routine heart operation had come out in isolation, the speculation about Blair's future would have been deafening. By pre-empting it, and throwing the press pack a bone about the new house, the story about the heart surgery came and went quickly.

At the White House, unpopular announcements are bundled together on a Friday to minimise their impact. Here's fictional *West Wing* spin doctor Josh explaining the process to his assistant:

Donna: What's 'take out the trash day'?

Josh: Friday.

Donna: I mean what is it?

Josh: Any stories we have to give the press that we're not wild about we give all in a lump on Friday.

Donna: Why do you do it in a lump?

Josh: Instead of one at a time?

Donna: I'd think you'd want to spread them out.

Josh: They've got X column inches to fill, right? They're gonna fill them no matter what.

Donna: Yes.

Josh: So if we give them one story, that story's X column inches.

Donna: And if we give them five stories ...

Josh: They're a fifth the size.

Donna: Why do you do it on Friday?

Josh: Because no one reads the paper on Saturday.

Donna: You guys are real populists, aren't you?

No 'no comment'

There is no such thing as 'no comment', and hoping a story will go away. Saying 'no comment' is the act of someone who watches too much television. It is as far removed from the real world of news as journalists with a label marked 'press' sticking out of the band in their hats, and people in newsrooms shouting 'hold the front page'.

To a journalist, 'no comment' means: 'the only comment I have to make is that I am guilty of something, have something to hide, or am engaged in a major cover-up, so you had better chase this story like your life depends on it'.

There can also be dangers in issuing straightforward denials, because the denial can provide a peg for the story ('So-and-so angrily denied reports last night that he was a heroin addict.')

The spin doctor must be able to comment and deal with adverse publicity as well as the good stuff. The best examples of 'crisis management' are when the polluting oil company or retailer caught selling poisonous cat food has been as open and honest as possible. Sometimes genuine contrition can turn a situation round, as we have seen with the Ashdown affair.

Be available

You often see the same names being quoted in newspapers and the same faces and voices on interviews. Is this because these people have special insights or knowledge which makes them more worthy of interview? No, it usually means that they were the first ones to agree to the bid. When programme-makers are looking for interviewees, they may phone round four or five people to fill one slot. Whoever comes back and says yes first gets the interview.

Next time, the researcher or producer might phone that person first of all to save time. If you say yes, and make yourself available at all hours of the day and night (and give good interviews), you will be asked again and again.

Honesty is the best policy

If journalists detect dishonesty or subterfuge, their trust will soon evaporate, and the game is up. There is no point whatever in lying to journalists. That is not to say that you have to tell the entire truth all the time, or let all the facts get in the way of a good story. Knowing which bits of the truth to reveal, when, and to whom, is the spin doctor's main skill.

The story of Home Secretary Jack Straw's son being arrested, back in 1997, is a good example of this. The sequence of events was roughly as follows: 17-year-old William Straw was targeted by two *Mirror* journalists who egged him on to purchase some cannabis. Before the story was revealed by the *Mirror*, Straw *pater* marched young William into the police station where he was arrested. The case them became *sub judice*, meaning that the identity of the son could not be revealed by the *Mirror*. Labour's spin doctors released the story of an unnamed cabinet minister behaving in a thoroughly responsible fashion in dealing with every middle-class parent's nightmare, but Straw's identity remained secret from the public. By the time the name of the minister was finally revealed, every journalist, politician and cognoscenti knew it was Straw because they had worked it out, so the impact was lessened. The sting was taken out of the story. By this daring strategy, Straw looked responsible and honest. The *Mirror* is painted as the villain. One of the journalists, Dawn Alford, was even arrested.

If Jack Straw had attempted to lie, to stonewall, to whitewash or cover-up, his cabinet career would have come to an abrupt and premature end.

Access to the organ grinder

Usually the spin doctor is the conduit for information between the journalist and a senior figure – or the 'sewer, not the sewage', as John Biffen once said of Bernard Ingham. Often the spin doctor acts as a lighting conductor for their boss, taking the flak and diverting criticism.

In the US, political spin doctors can even take part in public debates and media appearances themselves, as commentators in their own right. We have yet to see that development over here, thank heavens. (Although there are plenty of former spin doctors such as Bernard Ingham, Michael Shea, Amanda Platell, Martin Sixsmith and Charlie Whelan, who have cashed in their chips and become authors, columnists and pundits.)

But the practising spin doctor must not be a barrier, and from time to time must facilitate access to his or her boss for journalists. That means setting up briefings, lunches, news conferences, and private meetings for journalists. Journalists want to hear what the organ grinder has to say from time to time, not just listen to the chattering of the monkey.

Tricks that journalists play

I once asked a journalist about the trickery that journalists engage in to get a story. He replied sniffily: 'there is no trickery, just good journalism'. Whatever the definition, we can agree that journalists use a range of techniques to get a story – especially if someone doesn't want them to know it – ranging from simple psychological tricks to elaborate sting operations.

A good journalist can use cajolery, flattery, bribery and threats just as effectively as a good spin doctor. Naturally, the public never read about slippery hacks up to no good in their newspapers, because it is the slippery hacks that write them.

It is not for nothing that journalists in American political slang are known as 'scorps' (short for scorpions). Like their deadly namesakes, scorps have plenty of stings in their tail.

Here are some of the main techniques to watch out for:

'Would you say that …'

One of the oldest tricks in the book is the ascribing of quotes to individuals on the basis of a grunt of assent or a nod of the head. It runs as follows. The journalist says: 'Would you say that the redundancies your firm is making will devastate the community?' You reply: 'Yes in the short term, but in the medium term our £3 million retraining package will get people back to work.' Result? Headlines screaming 'DEVASTATION: firm predicts job loss chaos.'

I heard of a public relations consultant in the early stages of his career being tricked by a local paper over some client's misdemeanour. 'It's all been a bit of a cock-up, hasn't it?', suggested the hack. 'Well I suppose it must look like that, but the facts are …' replied our man. The local paper headline? One phrase, white out of black over half the front page: COCK-UP. This wasn't helped by the fact that the story concerned a local brewery, leading to the inevitable comments about organising a booze-up.

Be warned: anything a journalist says and you agree with, or even fail to disagree with, can be reported as your own words.

The best way to avoid the 'wouldn't you say …' trap is to categorically deny the views expressed, and offer something else instead. The fictional Prime Minister Francis Urquhart's way of dealing with it (if the journalist had got the right end of the stick) was to say 'You might say that, but I couldn't possibly comment'.

The Pinter pause

In a normal conversation, a pause in the flow of conversation is deemed a social embarrassment, and the natural inclination for most people is to fill the silence with something – anything, usually the first thing that comes into your head. Journalists use this natural inclination to trick people into saying more than they intended, or to stray off-message. It is important to remember that a broadcast interview, or a telephone call from a journalist, is not a normal conversation, and the usual social rules of engagement are suspended.

Lengthy Pinteresque silences from journalists are designed to make you blabber on and hopefully give something away. You should simply repeat your points over and over again. At a dinner party, endless repetition of the same point would be seen as a sign of crashing dullness or possibly mental instability. When dealing with journalists, it is a sign of professionalism and staying 'on-message.' Sometimes spin doctors' conversations with journalists can contain seemingly endless pauses, with each side waiting to see who cracks first.

Wood for the trees

One trick is for the journalist to decide what information they want, and disguise their true intentions in a forest of other questions. Usually this takes the form of lengthy questions about the interviewee's area of expertise, designed to lull them into a false sense of security, and the killer question is casually thrown in towards the end. When people complain about being quoted 'out of context' this is usually what they mean.

A variation on this approach is the *Columbo technique:* firing the killer question when your guard is down. Columbo, the 1970s' detective, would act like a bumbling dolt, and then deliver the killer question which tore apart the suspect's alibi with the preamble – 'there's just one thing bothering me …'. Journalists can use the same technique.

I know your boss

This is a straightforward bluff where the journalist implies that they already know the information they are after, so that the spin doctor inadvertently gives the game away. It can usually work if the hack pretends to be best mates with your boss, or your boss's boss, and to have received the information first-hand.

If in doubt, make it up …

Some journalists, in the absence of real information, simply make up quotes to back up their stories. Quotes can appear from 'sources close to …' or 'one backbencher said last night …', which could be anyone, and no one will ever know whether it was really said by a real person, or crafted by a harassed hack with a looming deadline.

Alastair Campbell blew the whistle on this practice in a piece in the *Mirror* on 3 July 2000: 'if you read about a senior insider, the place the insider is from is likely to be the journalist's head'.

How about this story from the *Sunday Mirror* (2 January 2005)?

> **Top Tories told to stay at home**
> Tory bosses have banned Shadow Ministers from campaign-ing round the country at the General Election. A Tory source revealed: 'We have to face up to the fact that most of our front bench are a liability.'

Who is the 'Tory source'? It could be anyone, from a backbench MP to the person who changes the toner cartridges at Conservative Central Office. I'm not suggesting for a moment that this quote or its source are fictional. The point is, we simply don't know.

Internal criticism from within an organisation can be invented, because no one will admit to it anyway, and quotes can usually be made up to substantiate stories about football transfers, Royal mar-riage rifts, and Cabinet rows. No one will ever know for sure.

Sometimes journalists go too far and spoil it for the rest. In 2003, *New York Times* journalist Jayson Blair was exposed as a fraud for making up quotes, eye-witness accounts and even whole stories.

Here's how *The Guardian* reported another faker at the *New York Times* – Jack Kelley – under the headline 'New "fake stories" row hits US media':

> Some of the details uncovered in the investigation of Kelley's work were truly astonishing. The paper examined Kelley's

claim to have been an eyewitness at a 2001 suicide bombing in Jerusalem. In his original copy Kelley had written that he saw three men have their heads blown off in the blast. In a first draft of his piece he described how the heads rolled 'with their eyes still blinking'. However, police records show that no adult victims of the blast were decapitated.

In another story Kelley visited Cuba in February 2002 and wrote a powerful piece describing a group of six refugees heading off to America in a boat. But, he claimed, a storm sank the craft a few days later and no one survived. Kelley produced a picture of a woman among the group called Yacqueline which was used along with the story. But far from dying at sea, she was tracked by the *USA Today* team alive and well and living in America. Her real name was Yamilet Fernández and she had worked at a hotel in Cuba before moving to America a year ago as a legal immigrant.

So don't believe everything you read in the newspapers, because your 'news' might be fiction.

Key points
- Your job is to supply news and views, and the media need you as much as you need them.
- Use a variety of techniques.
- Journalists have a full armoury of tricks, so watch out.
- Timing is everything.
- Sometimes journalists make stuff up.

Ways to stay on top

Take notes
All of the above proves that when you are dealing with journalists you should always take notes of the conversation. A journalist will have a note of the conversation, traditionally in shorthand on a reporters' notepad. Today it might easily be a Palm Pilot or similar device. Much time and effort was spent during the Hutton Inquiry looking at the records of conversations between Andrew Gilligan and Dr David Kelly held on the former's handheld computer, not a shorthand pad.

So it is worth having your own version as evidence for public inquiries, court cases, or simply disputes with the editor. Bernard Ingham, when working for Margaret Thatcher, kept a flawless shorthand note of almost every conversation he had with every journalist, official and politician he encountered, giving him huge powers of recall.

Contact-building
Spin doctoring is a contact sport, and contacts are the spin doctors' lifeblood. Spinning to a journalist with whom you have an ongoing relationship based on trust is much more likely to be successful than a 'cold call' to an unknown journalist. The spin doctor should nurture contacts with journalists, offer help and advice, give them occasional favours and special treatment, but always be prepared to challenge them, and complain to their editors.

Most of the time, your contact with journalists will be on the telephone. There are not many stories in the journalist's busy day that cannot be handled with a phone call, fax or email with extra information or a news release. If your contact with the journalist is likely to be ongoing, you might suggest a drink or lunch, or to meet up at a conference or event at which you will both be present.

If lunching with a journalist, it is a good idea to have some gossip or story ideas up your sleeve to make your guest feel that their time has not been wasted.

The process of holding on to and using contacts works well because journalists are trained to build their lists of useful sources of news and information, and that should include you. The spin doctor's contacts book is filled with the names of journalists, and the journalist's is filled with spin doctors.

Every time you speak to a journalist, you should log the call and make a record of their details. In co-ordinated PR campaigns, the frequency of calls from certain journalists can be a useful indicator of progress.

Building up your list of contacts, and keeping the contacts fresh, is a hugely valuable task. Most successful people are good at it. Harold Wilson was reputed to be able to remember the name of everyone he ever met.

Bill Clinton maintained card-index files in shoeboxes on every useful person he met from his college days onwards, until he became President of the United States. His biographer Martin Walker claims that:

> There was never a more assiduous maintainer of acquaintance and friendship than Clinton, and his political network was extraordinary … Names, addresses, phone numbers and birthdays, weddings and children, updated with new jobs and the latest publications, new meetings and family bereavements, they were all cross-referenced, with a note of any campaign contributions they had made.

When the cards were finally transferred on to computer, there were more than 10,000 files.

The importance of having 'contacts' can be overplayed. If your story is strong enough, and if you have something journalists want, it won't matter if you've never spoken before. Similarly, if your story is ropy, a journalist will not write it up simply because you bought them lunch. However, if a journalist needs a quote from a particular viewpoint, and there are a number of people and organisations capable of supplying the quote, the journalist will go for the one he or she knows best, and can be trusted to come up with a decent, punchy quote on the spot.

The contacts book is probably the most important tool of the trade. Tales abound of panic-stricken spin doctors who have realised their filofax or mobile has been stolen, or the power supply on their electronic organiser has failed and all data has been lost. The lesson of these disaster stories is to back up everything on computer, or photocopy all pages of the filofax or contacts book. You have been warned.

How to contact a journalist

As we have seen, journalists are busy, cynical and can often seem rude. At the national level they are fêted like film stars or cabinet ministers. So how can you contact your target journalist and get them to listen to your ideas? Here are some pointers.

Do your homework
Ensure that you are targeting the right person on the right publication or programme. Get their name right. Get the name of their programme or paper right. Investigate what issues interest them. Google them, and see if they've been in the news recently (awards, knighthoods, arrests for drink-driving, that kind of thing). Read what they've written recently, and perhaps be prepared to use a little flattery ('we've been following your articles on the national minimum wage, and love the way you've covered it …').

It is possible to get this spectacularly wrong. I once found myself at the bar drinking next to a prominent left-wing journalist. I told him how much I had enjoyed his recent article in *The Guardian* on the Liverpool dockers' strike. Thanks, he said, but that was written by someone else, and went back to his drink. End of conversation.

I once interviewed Denis Healey at his London flat for a magazine. The former Chancellor's opening line was how much he enjoyed my articles in *New Statesman*. Given how few articles I've ever had published in *New Statesman*, I was immensely flattered, right up until the point when I realised he thought I was Steve Richards, the *New Statesman*'s political editor. A few months later, Steve Richards told me that *he* had interviewed Denis Healey, and Healey thought Steve was me.

Have a story to tell

Do not waste their time. If you wonder why journalists sound harassed on the phone it is because of time-wasting PR people with pointless non-stories stopping them doing their work. So before you pick up the phone, make sure you have something useful to offer. If someone (an ignorant boss or pushy client) is pressurising you to phone up important journalists with a duff story, you should stand your ground, explain that annoying Paul Routledge might be counter-productive, and that your ability to do your job rests on your not looking like an amateur.

Choose the right method

There are basically four methods of contacting a journalist: by phone, by email, by letter, or in person. You can simultaneously try all four, but you might look like a stalker.

On the phone

If you are phoning a journalist you don't know, be ready to get to the point quickly. Say your name, organisation, and the purpose of the call straight away. Don't start by asking how they are, because the answer will be 'busy'. You should always ask if they have two or three minutes. If they are on a deadline, they won't be listening.

If they are too busy to take even a short call, ask when it would be convenient to phone back. Don't be fobbed off by them saying 'can you send a news release?' That's just their way of getting people off the phone. Try to get some level of commitment from them – to read the release and speak to you later. If you are rejected out of hand, don't take it personally.

By email

The *Daily Telegraph*'s George Jones once showed me his email inbox. On any day, he is sent hundreds of emails from hopeful press officers and organisations wanting his attention and to appear in his newspaper. What they all had in common was that he hadn't opened any of them. Sending an email is not the same as contacting a journalist, as they may not read it.

As a method of 'cold' contact, it is worse than useless. Think of the unsolicited emails you get sent by people trying to sell you cheap drugs, loans, mortgages and the opportunity for bigger body parts. Do you read them? Of course not. Email only really works effectively after you've made contact, to get information quickly to the journalist.

By letter

A letter can be more effective if it contains useful information or an invitation. It is harder to ignore, and places the request on the record.

In person

You may encounter journalists at conferences or seminars. Often organisations such as campaigning groups or think tanks invite journalists to chair meetings or seminars, or to contribute their wisdom to the event, and this often means that the event pops up in columns or news reports. Big events often have a 'media partner' to serve as sponsor, which means guaranteed coverage.

If you see a journalist you want to talk to at an event, you should summon up your courage and make a personal introduction. Have a business card ready. Ask them if you can follow up the conversation with a phone call. Don't corner them and bend their ear, because they'll resent it. Definitely don't do what a former press office colleague of mine did when she wanted to attract the attention of Richard Branson: she tipped a glass of wine on his feet.

How to handle an unexpected call from a journalist

Often journalists phone up organisations seeking confirmation of a story, leak or tip-off they've received. If you, or someone in your organisation, gets a call they're not expecting from a journalist, they may catch you off guard. The result may be a quote or confirmation of a damaging story. So you need a strategy to handle these kinds of calls. First, you need to establish who the call is from – their name, news organisation, and what they want. Journalists can phone companies or public bodies and say they are 'customers' or 'citizens', which is technically true. If they say they are 'working on a story for the *Mirror*' it might mean they are a freelance hoping to sell the story to the *Mirror*. So you need to take their details and phone back to check their credentials. Check what their deadline is. Ask if they will put their questions in an email. In short, don't be drawn into giving off-the-cuff quotes; take control of the conversation and buy some time for yourself.

The journalist's job is to keep you on the phone for as long as possible, using every type of cajolery and incessant questioning. You need a stock phrase up your sleeve to get them off the line. Explain that you will get back to them with a quote, but you need time to formulate it, and the longer the journalist keeps you on the line, the longer it will take to come back. Be firm. Put the phone down. And be sure to keep your promise to come back by the deadline, or you may find that your quote in the story is 'refused to comment'.

Be a funnel, not a sieve

From the smallest community campaign to the largest corporation, there must be a single point of contact for journalists. Calls and enquiries must be funnelled through to a central point, where skilled press officers can deal with the media. If your organisation is full of holes like a sieve, you will find it impossible to control the flow of information. Stories will leak out. People will give unhelpful quotes to the media. You will look like a shambles. Every journalist is trained to look for weak spots in the PR façade – disgruntled employees, annoyed contractors, off-guard directors. One wheeze is for journalists to hang around outside large organisations' HQs where all the smokers congregate and pretend to be a member of staff. No one really knows everyone in a large organisation, so who's to know that the guy handing round the Silk Cut and asking about the big moves on the 14th floor is really from the *Financial Times*?

Many organisations have a protocol on who is allowed to talk to the media, and all staff are instructed what to do if they get a call. *In some places, it is a sacking offence to talk to journalists.*

Write like a journalist

Journalism is one of the last bastions of decent English, where proper attention is given to spelling, grammar, punctuation and style. Spin doctors should adopt the same scrupulous approach.

The first set of rules concerns basic good grammar, punctuation and spelling. If you seek to communicate you should take the time to learn when to write 'fewer' and when to write 'less', the difference between metaphor and similie, how to spell 'millennium', 'noticeable' and 'resuscitate', and when to use a semi-colon. And you should have noticed that I misspelled 'simile'.

The second set of rules concerns 'house style'. These are the self-imposed rules for writing which an organisation uses to cover all the grey areas not covered by formal grammar and spelling. House-style rules should cover the use of accents on foreign words, Americanisms, capitals or lower case, captions, dates, numbers, foreign words, places, names, government and politics, hyphens, initials, italics, jargon, measures, and spelling.

These rules can differ from organisation to organisation. I worked in a press office where the use of capital letters was all but outlawed, even for titles like 'secretary of state'. The next place I worked insisted on capitals for titles, even 'Refuse Collector'. So you have to learn the rules, and then stick to them. If charged with establishing house style for your organisation, you can do worse than buying an established style guide, for example the *FT Style Guide,* and adopt that.

Language must be tailored to the purpose in hand, and this is particularly true of dealing with the media. News releases must emulate in style and content the newspapers at which they are targeted. Feature articles must flow like the articles in that day's papers. They must appear to be crying out for inclusion. It must be easy for the journalist to turn your news release into copy which his subs will accept.

The best advice comes from one of the last century's best writers, George Orwell:

> A scrupulous writer, in every sentence he writes, will ask himself at least four questions, thus: 'What am I trying to say? What words will express it? What image or idiom will make it clearer? Is this image fresh enough to have an effect?' And he will probably ask himself two more: 'Could I put it more simply? Have I said anything avoidably ugly?'

There are plenty of books on the market which tell you how to write proper English, from journalism textbooks such as Wynford Hick's *English for Journalism* and *Subediting for Journalists* by Wynford Hicks and Tim Holmes, to books such as Lynne Truss's unlikely best-seller on punctuation, *Eats, Shoots and Leaves*.

You should give attention to getting your spelling, grammar and punctuation right, because it shows that you know what you're doing. There are also journalistic conventions which you should obey. Here are some useful pointers:

Spelling
There are many words which are frequently misspelled. Here are some of the more common ones (according to Wynford Hicks in his excellent *English for Journalists*). If you get more than 20 out 25 correct, you are a genius:

Abhorrence
Annihilate
Authoritative
Connoisseur
Corroborate
Definitely
Descendant
Embarrass
Fallacious
Harass
Innocuous
Jeopardise
Liaison
Mantelpiece
Minuscule
Noticeable
Omitted
Pseudonym

Reconnaissance
Restaurateur
Resuscitate
Supersede
Targeted
Unforeseen
Vacillate

Most people's problem (apart from not being able to spell diffi-cult words, which is forgivable) is relying on their computer's spell-checker, which is American and no use at all. The answer lies, I'm afraid, in buying a dictionary and looking words up. Even after the most rigorous process of editing, checking and re-reading, the occasional spelling mistake may appear – no one is infallible!

Punctuation

An overused punctuation mark in spin doctoring is the exclama-tion mark (!). I think using exclamation marks (known in journal-ism as 'screamers') to try to make your text look more exciting than it is is the same as laughing at your own jokes. If what you're saying is remarkable, interesting, shocking or funny, then you don't need an exclamation mark. If it isn't, then !!!! will make no difference.

Perhaps the most notorious item of punctuation is the apos-trophe, which causes the teachers, journalists and academics who know how to use them to look down at the builders, grocers and café owners who don't. Apostrophes are used for two things: to show possession (that something belongs to someone) or omission (that something is missing.)

The apostrophe changes position to show singular or plural. So the mat belonging to the cat is:

The cat's mat

If there's more than one cat, the apostrophe moves place:

The cats' mat

It doesn't matter how many mats there are.

The problem comes when there are complications. One complication is when the word ends with an 's'. So the park belonging to St James can be St James' Park or St James's Park. The pamphlet by Hazel Blears is Hazel Blears' pamphlet or Hazel Blears's pamphlet. It is absolutely never Hazel Blear's.

The other complication is 'its' and 'it's', because this is the exception to the rule. When you want to use a short form of 'it is' ('it's Friday tomorrow') you use 'it's'. The apostrophe shows that the 'i' is missing. When you want to show something belonging to 'it', you use 'its' without an apostrophe. So that's all clear then.

Numbers

A useful thing to know is how journalists treat numbers. From one to ten, the number is spelt out with letters. From 11 onwards, the numbers are written in numerals. The exception to the rule is if a number starts the sentence, when it is usually spelt out in letters. In headlines, you can use numerals to fit the space.

Clichés

You should avoid clichés like the plague.

You should avoid acid test, bitter end, burning issue, crying need, dead as a dodo, dark horse, horns of a dilemma, last but not least, sea of faces, take the bull by the horns, or this day and age.

If you can't give clichés a wide berth, steer clear of them, and avoid them like the plague, then rope in some other Joe to put pen to paper.

How about this string of clichés from David Mellor, writing in the *Evening Standard* sports pages about Alex Ferguson: 'Now he is the biter bit perhaps he'll change his tune, but I'm not holding my breath.' Placing three clichés in one sentence must be some kind of record.

Jargon

Every organisation or profession uses its own jargon, short hand and acronyms. Jargon can be used by members of the same profession or interest as a way of speeding up communication, and as a method of excluding outsiders from the group. This is true of journalists, politicians, doctors, lawyers, and the military, not to mention plumbers, darts players, war gamers and taxi-drivers.

The corporate world is full of it: face time; run it up the flag-pole and see who salutes it; I'll get my people to talk to your people; I've got a window on the 26th; total quality management; down- and right-sizing; brainstorming session.

Because jargon by its nature is exclusionary, it should never find its way into the communication between a spin doctor and his audiences. Once again, George Orwell's advice is the best:

> Never use a long word when a short one will do, and never use jargon if you can think of an everyday English equivalent.

This is from a real news release:

> Repeated Methods Ltd today announced that it has grown exponentially in 1992, and that this accelerating rate of adoption has firmly established their Fractal Transform technology as a de-facto standard for still image compression.

It is the use of Latin which most amuses me in this good example of a news release destined for the bin.

This is from a letter I intercepted before it was sent from a local council to residents:

> As part of a series of measures intended to help revitalise your local town centre, the council will construct entry treatments at the above locations.

And what exactly do you think an entry treatment is? It sounds vaguely medical, and certainly unpleasant. This letter was actually telling local people and businesses that roadworks were about to disrupt their lives, make them late for work, lose them customers, and generally make life miserable. The letter made things worse. Your communications should never be part of the problem you are trying to solve.

Acronyms and initials

What's the difference? An acronym is a word made from initials which is pronounced as a new word – for example radar, UNESCO, or DEFRA. Initials are shorthand for a longer series of words, but each letter is enunciated, for example BBC, WTO, GMB, or ODPM. If the initials are very well known (BBC) you can get away with using them. If not, you should spell out the name in full the first time you use it, and then use the initials from then on. Never use initials without explaining them, especially if they have more than one meaning:

PR – public relations, proportional representation
PC – politically correct, police constable, personal computer
FSA – Financial Services Authority, Food Standards Agency

I pity the US Army spin doctor who had to explain this piece of nonsense uttered by General Schwarzkopf during the first Gulf War: 'It is not yet possible to get clear BDA in this area of the KTO. The continued presence of Tripe A means a constant risk of allied personnel becoming KIA or WIA.'

Proofreading

Proofreading is a real skill, because it involves reading text in a different way to a normal reader. Instead of reading for meaning, you are reading to spot mistakes. The problem is that your brain often corrects mistakes as you read a piece of text, and you read what you assume is there, not what is actually there. This means that glaring errors can be missed.

This email popped uninvited into my inbox, and it makes the point rather well:

> I cdnuolt blveiee taht I cluod aulaclty uesdnatnrd waht I was rdanieg.
>
> The phaonmneal pweor of the hmuan mnid. Aoccdrnig to a rscheearch at Cmabrigde Uinervtisy, it deosn't mttaer inwaht oredr the ltteers in a wrod are, the olny iprmoatnt tihng is taht the frist and lsat ltteer be in the rghit pclae. The rset can be a taotl mses and you can sitll raed it wouthit a porbelm. Tihs is bcuseae the huamn mnid deos not raed ervey lteter by istlef, but the wrod as a wlohe. Amzanig huh? yaeh and I awlyas thoughtslpeling was ipmorantt!

No wonder proofreading is hard. A useful trick is to read the text from back to front, looking for spelling mistakes or the same word appearing twice. Another trick is to get someone else to do it for you.

Editing

Editing someone else's work is a skill involving both craftsmanship and diplomacy. Professional writers are used to working with editors, but most people don't like seeing their work edited; some take it personally. Editing takes place for a variety of reasons – to fit the space, to conform to house style, or to correct errors.

An editor should never edit to change the meaning of an article, or remove substantive points without consultation with the writer. The spin doctor often finds themselves in the situation of editing a client's work, which must be handled with great tact and diplomacy, because prominent figures often think they can write well, and usually don't like criticism.

Common mistakes

You should try to get things right. Offering such advice is of course a huge hostage to fortune. I know that everything I've ever written has contained mistakes. When knocking out news releases which invariably contained some howler, I would point out that my news releases were like genuine Persian rugs: they always contained a deliberate flaw, because only Allah is perfect.

The first edition of this book was so full of errors that my mother (a teacher with 40-odd years' experience) was tempted to take a red pen to it. I'm sure a close read of this edition would show up errors of spelling, punctuation and grammar, even after a rigorous proofreading process.

Every fact that you use must be correct. It's worth checking everything twice, because a factual error undermines your case and will haunt you for months, as Education Minister Stephen Byers found out when he gave the wrong answer to seven times eight, and Dan Quayle will never forget when he told schoolchildren that 'potato' had an 'e' at the end.

There are common errors which you should try to avoid, and feel smug about spotting in others' work. Here are my favourites:

King Canute is not an example of someone who thought he was all-powerful; he knew he couldn't stop the waves by his command, and was proving it to his courtiers.

The *Mother of Parliaments* refers to England, not the House of Commons.

It is the *love of money*, not money per se, that is the root of all evil.

Frankenstein is not the name of the monster, but of its creator.

You cannot have more than two *alternatives*. The word means one thing or another. Any more than two, and it becomes options or choices.

Champagne comes from the Champagne region of France. Other places make fizzy white wine: Australia, California, Hungary. But this is not champagne.

Crescendo is a musical term meaning the swell and rise of a piece of music to an apex of emotion or volume. It does not mean the pinnacle itself. So nothing can 'rise to a crescendo'; the crescendo is the rise. For example, when Polly Toynbee reported in *The Guardian* that William Hague's speech to the 1999 Tory conference was 'a remarkable piece of narrow nationalism, rising to a crescendo of Europhobia', she meant that the speech had a crescendo reaching a peak of Europhobia.

Decimate means to remove one in ten. So nine-tenths of a population, workforce or species which is 'decimated' remains untouched and stands a good chance of survival. Strictly speaking, the spokesperson for Farmers for Action who was reported in *The Guardian* on 26 April 2005 complaining that British agriculture 'is being decimated and there is no future for youngsters in the industry' should be grateful that nine-tenths of his industry still survives.

Gambit means the opening move in chess. You can't have a closing or middle gambit. Gambits are always at the opening of play. So 'opening gambit' is a tautology. Here's Nancy Banks-Smith on 9 April 2005 in *The Guardian* reviewing an episode of Coronation Street: 'And Deirdre, after a promising opening gambit ("I am so sorry! I am so very sorry!") that led us to hope she had thought better of the whole business, just went on and on and on.'

Protagonist means the main character or actor in a story or drama. To talk of 'the main protagonist' is just plain wrong.

Even William Rees-Mogg, writing in *The Times* on 16 May 2005, was incorrect when he wrote (describing a plot inside the 1950s' Labour Party) 'except for Bevan, all the main protagonists came from Oxford'. I bet the subs didn't dare correct him.

Unique: if something is one of a kind, it is unique. If not then it isn't. It cannot be almost unique, or virtually unique. Tony Blair is quoted in *The Guardian* on 18 June 2003 as saying that having the Lord Chancellor act as Speaker in the Lords is 'virtually unique'. Well, is it or isn't it unique?

Light years measure distance, not time.

Bonus means an additional benefit. You don't need to say an 'added bonus.'

As you might guess, I don't get invited to many dinner parties.

Key points
- Take notes of your conversations with journalists so you can correct mistakes afterwards and challenge their recollection.
- Build a file of contacts, keep it updated, and back it up.
- Contact journalists in ways which make it more likely they will use your story.
- Beware unexpected calls from journalists, and have a strategy for dealing with them.
- Write like a journalist.
- Cut out jargon, slang, technical language and explain initials and acronyms.
- Avoid mistakes where possible.

Chapter Five
In the News or in the Bin?

Always always always tell the story through people.

Arthur Christiansen

Technique is never enough on its own. You need a good story to sell. Where people often go wrong is in assuming that what's interesting to them will be interesting to a journalist. Your story may be worthy – but is it newsworthy?

Successful journalists have an instinct for what makes a good story. They can sniff one out like a truffle-hound. Some might argue that this instinctive nose for a story cannot be taught: you either have the talent or you don't. Arthur McEwan, editor of the *San Francisco Examiner,* said that 'news is whatever a good editor chooses to print'. But journalists are also influenced by commercial imperatives, and the political slant of the publication. Papers have to be sold. Proprietors' prejudices have to be pandered to. Journalism can never be purely objective – there is always a context.

The first criterion is that news is only news if it is reported. On Boxing Day 2004 an earthquake in the Indian Ocean created tsunami waves which wiped out thousands of miles of coastline from Thailand to Somalia, and killed tens of thousands of people. On each of the hundreds of beaches affected by the walls of water were individual stories of heroism and tragedy: brave rescues, families destroyed, and lucky escapes. But in only a handful of cases were these stories told through the media. This doesn't make the untold stories any less heroic or tragic. But without a journalist there to report the events, there is no story. This is particularly true in television news: no pictures, no story.

On any day of the year the newspapers and broadcasters have more news than space available. Choices must be made and judgements applied. Reporters decide the two or three stories on which to focus their efforts, and editors decide which ten or twenty stories will ultimately appear. Even if a reporter has written a story, the editor may choose not to let it appear. In the days of hot metal, the paper bearing the story would have been placed on a metal spike – hence the expression 'spiked', meaning dropped or unused.

One view of 'what is news' is offered by the international news agency Reuters:

> Fires, explosions, floods … railway accidents, destructive storms, earthquakes, shipwrecks … accidents … street riots … strikes … the suicide of persons of note, social or political, and murders of a sensational or atrocious character.

That was issued by Reuters in 1883.

Organisations run on budgets, reports, committee decisions, strategies and targets – but journalism is about people. Editor Arthur Christiansen advised his staff: 'always always always tell the story through people'.

Fleet Street legend Harold Evans said: 'News is people. It is people talking and people doing. Committees and Cabinets and courts are people; so are fires, accidents and planning decisions. They are only news because they involve and affect people.'

So a spin doctor has to turn budgets, reports and committee decisions into stories about people – who's happy, who's sad, who's up and who's down? What do people think and feel? What are they saying and doing?

How can the spin doctor persuade a journalist that their story is news? An analysis of news stories in print and broadcast can help us understand the types of stories which appear. By understanding the media we are targeting we can mould the information we have into a form which a journalist will recognise and find interesting. If you start from the premise that your story is worthy and interesting, and that a journalist should be motivated by the same things you are, you are probably going to fail. The trick of dealing with the media is to craft your stories into formats and styles which match your target media as closely as possible.

One useful test to apply to your stories is the 'Hey Doris' test, used by *Sun* journalist Wendy Henry during the 1980s, when the Currant Bun was edited by Kelvin MacKenzie. Unless a story might provoke a *Sun* reader to exclaim to her friend: 'Hey Doris, take a look at this …', the story didn't make it into the paper.

For most stories which we might offer to journalists we should be aiming to pass the 'so what?' test. Journalists, like the rest of us, have a broad understanding of what organisations do and how the world works. So if your story contains nothing more interesting that 'charity raises funds', 'politician makes speech', 'business holds sale', 'public services provide services to the public' or 'football team plays football', then don't be disappointed if the reaction to your story is 'so what?' A surprising number of news releases sent to journalists, brimming with news of 'groundbreaking developments' in tractor technology or the latest thoughts of a middle manager in the frozen dessert business to the 'Puddings 2020' conference in Harrogate, fail this simple test.

As we shall see, part of the spin doctor's art lies in taking the mundane and commonplace and turning it into something unusual and newsworthy.

News values

At the heart of any engaging news story is one or more of the following news values. News values are what make a story newsworthy. Journalists are taught news values at college, but once they start work and the relentless tyranny of the deadline takes over, they become instinctive. If you boil down every story in today's newspapers and broadcasts, they will contain one or more of these 'news values.'

Novelty

'Novelty' comes from the Latin adjective 'novus', which translates as 'new', 'young', or 'fresh'. News stories have to contain news – something which we are reading or hearing for the first time. They have to add to the recipient's stock of knowledge.

There is a famous journalism adage that: 'dog bites man, that's not news. But man bites dog – now *that's* news.' This means that for a story to be newsworthy it should contain something surprising, counter-intuitive and challenging. If a dog bites a man, we think, 'so what? Dogs bite men all the time.' But if a man bites a dog, we want to know why. We want to know who the man was, where it happened, why he did it and how he felt afterwards.

This story from the *Daily Telegraph* (13 January 2005) is pure 'man bites dog':

Struggling Bath spa runs out of ... water
The ill-fated Bath Spa, which was intended to turn Britain's only natural hot springs into a major tourist attraction, received another blow yesterday: it has run out of water.

Or this, from the *Daily Telegraph* (4 February 2005):

Judge passes sentence by mobile phone
A taxi driver has become the first person to be sentenced by an English court in a call to his mobile phone.

Here's the *Independent on Sunday* (6 February 2005):

No time, gentlemen, please: is this UK's first 24-hour pub?
The Rainbow pub stands next to a steel-shuttered warehouse on a noisy arterial road which links the centre of Birmingham to its outlying suburban sprawl. The pub offers its customers – a mix of die-hard drinkers and trendy urbanites – live music, dancing

and a set menu. But the Rainbow is no ordinary venue: it is set to be one of the first pubs in Britain to offer round-the-clock drinking under a controversial change in licensing laws.

Oddity

Moving on from novelty, we come to the next news value: oddity. Something can be new without being odd. But oddity gives us a new dimension. In the tabloids, this can stray into the lurid, shocking, weird or just plan sickening.

The broadsheets are not immune; for example, see this from the *Daily Telegraph* (31 December 2004):

67-year-old retired teacher is expecting twin girls
A 67-year-old retired Romanian university teacher is seven months' pregnant with twins after almost a decade of treatment in fertility clinics, doctors reported yesterday.

Or this, from the same edition:

Seaman has breast surgery on the Navy
The Royal Navy has paid for two sailors – one of them a man – to have cosmetic breast surgery. As the Armed Forces face budget cuts, it was disclosed yesterday that the man had had breast reduction surgery and the woman implants.

Here's *The Sun* (13 January 2005):

Billy the Real Fish
Remind you of anyone? This fish with an amazing human face should be on Catch of the Day. It looks half-man, half-fish – just like goalkeeper Billy the Fish in the comic magazine *Viz*.

Conflict

All kinds of stories are written up as conflicts: politics, sport, business, celebrities and campaigns. There is little room in journalism for nuance or subtlety – stories are often conflated into one side bashing the hell out of the other. Just think of the thousands of words dedicated to these conflicts over the years: Israelis versus Palestinians, Blur versus Oasis, Irish nationalists versus unionists, Gordon Brown versus Tony Blair, Manchester United versus Arsenal, foxhunt supporters versus opponents, and on and on.

How about this from *The Observer* (9 January 2005)?

> **Blair-Brown feud out of control over new claims**
> Gordon Brown has been sidelined from Labour's election campaign because Blairites fear his supporters could sabotage it, it emerged last night as the civil war between the two men plunged to new depths.

Here's *The Guardian* from 27 January 2005:

> **Democrats divided over rethink on abortion**
> The Democratic party, shaken by its loss on 'moral values' in last November's elections, has embarked on a rethink of its approach to the core issue of abortion rights.

The Sun on 16 May 2005 reported on:

> **Utd fans' cup war**
> Fans furious at American tycoon Malcolm Glazier's takeover of Manchester United plan to wreck Saturday's FA Cup final with protests.

Journalists on local papers like campaigns led by local residents, parents, businesses, etc., especially if the target is the town hall or government. Here's the *Watford Observer* on 13 May 2005:

> **Development protesters pledge to stop bulldozers**
> Residents facing a seven-storey development on their doorsteps have said they will lie in the path of any bulldozers which come on the land.

If you can build elements of conflict into your story – with challenges, demands, criticisms or protests against your opponents – it has a greater chance of being picked up by a journalist.

Scandal

We all love watching the rich and powerful come a cropper, and a good scandal can keep journalists busy for weeks. Scandals come in two basic forms: financial (people stealing money or things from other people) and sexual (people doing things with other people they shouldn't be doing). Sometimes there are drugs involved too. Some newspapers, especially the *News of the World*, specialise in scandals and have teams of reporters armed with open chequebooks looking for next week's front-page victim. What makes a scandal story more potent are the lengths the victim goes to to protect their reputation. If they lie or stonewall, it usually ends up being worse for them.

A great irony of the John Major years is that whilst all around him the sky was dark with the flurry of ministers' resignation letters, his own affair with Edwina Currie remained a secret until a decade later. Even then it was not discovered by a journalist, but by Edwina Currie publishing her lamentable diary.

What the newspaper considers a scandal may not always strike a chord with the reader. When businessmen, footballers, or politicians are caught doing something up to no good, many of us just shrug our shoulders and say 'so what?' On other occasions, you wonder what on earth they were thinking. If you were advising Prince Harry on what to wear to a fancy dress party, would you steer him away from the Afrika Korps uniform? Perhaps the Charlie Chaplin, Darth Vader, or comedy gorilla might have been a better choice. In the absence of a sensible spin doctor's counsel, here's the mess he landed himself in on 13 January 2005 in *The Sun*:

HARRY THE NAZI
Prince's swastika outfit at party
Prince Harry stuns partygoers by attending a pal's birthday bash dressed as a Nazi soldier.

The Guardian also covered this story on its front page in later editions on the same day:

Royal family caught up in Nazi row
Clarence House was last night forced into a major damage-limitation exercise after Prince Harry was pictured in Nazi uniform at a fancy-dress party.

Often what a newspaper considers a scandal reflects the paper's own cultural values. Here's the *Evening Standard*'s front-page story from 12 January 2005:

Cookery exams outrank physics
A distinction in cake decorating ranks ahead of an A-grade in GCSE physics in new school league tables.

Here's the *Independent on Sunday* (6 February 2005):

Sleaze and Archer haunt Howard
The spectre of Tory sleaze loomed up from the past to haunt Michael Howard this weekend as Lord Archer became eligible to rejoin his former party.

What about this story in the *Sunday Times* on 15 May 2005?

Royal Mail boss paid £3m
Adam Crozier, chief executive of Royal Mail, was paid almost £3m last year, despite a rise in complaints over late, lost and stolen letters.

Is it a real scandal for a leading businessman to receive such a large salary? It depends on where the reader draws the line.

In the later chapter on dealing with a crisis, we shall look at how a spin doctor should react when a scandal hits.

Tragedy (and triumph over tragedy)
Tragedies get reported, from major events like earthquakes, fires, hijackings, bomb blasts and sinking ships, to individual tales of tragedy like freak accidents, murders, cancer, drowning, and car crashes. Some editions of newspapers are packed with tragedies to the point where you wonder if it's safe to leave the house.

This is from *The Sun* (3 January 2005):

> **Pals see lad of 12 drown in boat fall**
> A boy from a rowing club drowned yesterday after his boat tipped up in a freezing river.

And this is from the *Daily Telegraph* (10 January 2005):

> **Flood misery for gale-lashed Britain**
> Five people were feared dead and thousands were left homeless after floods and gales cut a trail of devastation across northern parts of Britain and Ireland at the weekend.

A journalistic twist on straightforward human misery is the triumph-over-tragedy story (or ToT for short), which is often a heart-warming tale of human sacrifice and courage which might serve to persuade you that there's hope for the human race after all. For example, this is from the *Daily Telegraph* (31 December 2004):

> **Rich and poor unite in world's greatest charitable mission**
> The scenes of devastation and death from Asia have triggered the biggest, and speediest, fund-raising appeal in modern history.

Or this from the *Sunday Express* (2 January 2005):

> **'Miracle' in the rubble**
> A survivor has been dragged from the rubble after being buried for more than five days. Ichsan Azmi, 27, was found by an

Indonesian search-and-rescue team in the city of Banda Aceh late on Friday.

This was in *The Guardian* (12 January 2005):

Man says he survived at sea for two weeks by eating coconuts
A tsunami survivor says he drifted on the Indian Ocean for two weeks, living on coconuts that he prised open with his teeth while floating on pieces of wood, a broken boat, and finally a fishing raft.

Celebrity

We live in a society obsessed by celebrity. You are imbued with newsworthiness by the very act of appearing on television or in the tabloids. It becomes a self-fulfilling act: you are famous for being famous. In recent years, so-called 'reality' television shows, with Channel 4's *Big Brother* as the glittering exemplar, have created a stream of famous-for-five-minutes demi-celebs. Add to these blink-and-you'll-miss-them oddballs the serious celebrities – actors, writers, newsreaders, ministers, comedians, artists, sportsmen and women, royals, pop stars and television presenters – and you have a whole universe of celebrity. The addition of celebrity is like sprinkling magic newsworthiness dust over a story. Celebrity transforms the mundane into the magical.

This story in the *News of the World* (2 January 2005) is a perfect example of a celebrity story. Lots of people catch pneumonia every winter. But when a famous footballer catches it, it makes it into the paper:

Gazza agony
Soccer legend Paul Gascoigne was gravely ill in hospital last night with pneumonia. The hell-raising former England star, 37, collapsed at home and had to be rushed into medical care.

Or this story in *The Sun* (3 January 2005) about a man driving too fast in an expensive car. Not a story? It is when the man is Pierce Brosnan:

Brosnan terror in 95mph car race
Former Bond hero Pierce Brosnan has told how he got lured into a deadly car race with a macho young driver.

Or this from the same edition:

Denise quits panto after breakdown
Former Corrie star Denise Welch has pulled out of a panto after suffering a 'complete breakdown'.

Stories about failed coups in far-away places might make a couple of paragraphs in the overseas news section of a broadsheet. But when the son of a Prime Minister is implicated, it's front-page news. This is from *The Guardian* (13 January 2005):

Thatcher pleads guilty to coup role
Sir Mark Thatcher will plead guilty in a South African court today to being involved in the failed attempt to stage a coup in Equatorial Guinea, according to legal sources.

These stories are only 'news' because they concern celebrities. No celebrity, no story.

Danger
Danger in journalism comes in all shapes and sizes: health scares, killers on the loose, faulty electrical goods, factory closures, terrorist threats to the water supplies, economic downturns, carcinogenic foodstuffs, deadly new viruses, and so on. Danger is a news value which is reflected in stories about dangers to the community, or to the individual. Here are some examples:

The *Daily Telegraph* (4 January 2005) warns:

Doctors say 24-hour opening will worsen drink 'epidemic'

Britain is suffering from an epidemic of alcohol-related problems, with one in 20 people dependent on drink and as many at serious risk of liver disease, the Royal College of Physicians said yesterday.

This article in *The Guardian* (13 January 2005) is a great example of a story placed by a charity to promote its issue and cause, but which is published on its merits as a newsworthy story:

Britons' cancer ignorance

Britons show alarming ignorance about cancer and the way in which they could change their lifestyles to dramatically reduce their risk of contracting it, the charity Cancer Research UK said yesterday.

The *Daily Telegraph*'s front page on 13 January 2005 had this warning:

Don't allow under-9s to use a mobile

And children up to 14 should only make short calls, warns radiation watchdog

Children under the age of nine should not use mobile phones because of potential health risks, the Government's leading adviser on radiation said yesterday.

This is from *The Guardian* (10 January 2005):

Pesticides may cause prostate cancer, say government advisers

Government cancer advisers have for the first time said pesticides, particularly weed-killers, might cause prostate cancer and want better monitoring of their use, *The Guardian* has learned.

And what about this headline from the *Maidenhead Advertiser* (13 May 2005)?

Police hunt sex pest
Police believe a pervert who sexually assaulted a 13-year-old girl in Gringer Hill may have preyed on women in the area for years.

Milestones
Milestones help make sense of a story. We can understand the point of a story if there is a chunky number attached to it. A story about Labour's City Academies is obscure to most people. But a headline such as this one from *The Guardian* on 13 January 2005, with a clear milestone ('half'), helps make sense of it:

Half of flagship academies fail to lift results
The government's programme to spend hundreds of millions of pounds replacing failing inner-city schools with privately backed academies has had limited success, according to figures published today.

Or this from the *Norwich Evening News* (4 February 2005):

Repossessions jump by 20% in Norwich
Hundreds of families face losing their homes as the number of repossession orders rockets in Norwich.

Anniversaries
It seems obvious, but every year contains the first, fifth, tenth, 50th, 100th and 200th anniversary of historical events, battles, treaties, and famous people's deaths and births. So that creates endless opportunities for articles. Editors like anniversary stories because they can be planned for in advance, graphics departments and picture desks can scour the archives, and writers can have time to consider their angles and do their homework.

So an editor or writer might think: what's coming up in 2005? Here's a random selection of anniversaries:

It's ten years since Nick Leeson brought down Barings Bank, the bombing in Oklahoma, the OJ Simpson trial, the assassination of Yitzhak Rabin, the death of comic legend Peter Cook.

It's 20 years since the end of the miners' strike, Mohammed Al-Fayed's takeover of Harrods, the first television broadcast of the House of Lords, the start of Gorbachev's leadership in the USSR, the release of the disastrous 'New Coke', the Live Aid concert, and the death of Orson Welles.

It's 40 years since the death of Winston Churchill, the first US troops arriving in Vietnam, the Post Office Tower opening in London, the first showing of *The Sound of Music*, the birth of Sarah Jessica Parker, and the death of T. S. Eliot.

It's 60 years since the atomic bombing of Nagasaki and Hiroshima, the end of the Second World War, the Nuremberg Trials, the election of the Attlee Labour Government, and the birth of Rod Stewart, Eric Clapton, and Van Morrison.

It's 100 years since the foundation of Las Vegas, the birth of Christian Dior, Albert Speer and Greta Garbo, the first U-boat, Norwegian independence, mutiny on the Battleship *Potemkin*, and Einstein's work on relativity.

It's 200 years since the first-ever trooping of the colour, the Lewis and Clark expedition, the Battle of Austerlitz, the Battle of Trafalgar and the death of Horatio Nelson, and the birth of Hans Christian Andersen.

These anniversaries provide journalists with limitless ideas for articles, features, documentaries and interviews. The 60th anniversary of the liberation of Auschwitz led to articles and programmes, including this story in *The Observer* (9 January 2005):

Sixty years on, Nazi death camp's new tale of horror
Eva Mozes Kor learnt on her first night at Auschwitz what the
smoke billowing from the chimneys meant: that most of her
family had been killed.

Or this from *The Times* (13 January 2005):

70 and dead, but Elvis is king of the charts again
The king of Rock 'n' Roll reigns at the top of the charts once
again, marking what would have been Elvis Presley's 70th
birthday.

Here's the *Wandsworth Borough News* (2 February 2005) making a
story out of thin air:

One year on, death of Kofi, 18, still a mystery
One year since the mysterious death of a teenager on a rail-
way line, police have said the circumstances that led to a body
being found on the tracks remain unclear.

For the spin doctor, anniversaries present opportunities to piggy-
back stories which you know are going to come up. Your own
organisation might have its own anniversaries.

This is a good example of a charity creating news from an anniversary, taken from the BBC Online website (12 January 2005):

Barnardo's then and now
Children's charity Barnardo's has produced a report marking
100 years since its founder, Dr Thomas Barnardo, died.

Superlatives
Journalists love the biggest, smallest, longest, and fattest. Not the
second biggest, mark you. The biggest. Superlatives can lift a story
from the mundane to the newsworthy. The man who collected
the biggest ball of string, the dog with the longest ears, the oldest
woman to give birth – these are newsworthy.

Here's a grim one from *The Guardian* (27 January 2005):

Bloodiest day for US as violence grows

The US suffered its worst day in Iraq since the war began when a Marine helicopter crashed in the western desert and insurgents launched a new wave of attacks, leaving a total of 37 Americans dead.

Or this from the *Independent on Sunday* (6 February 2005):

Longest-ruling leader dies

Africa's longest-serving ruler, President Gnassingbe Eyadema of Togo, 69, died after ruling for 38 years.

Factor X

If you are concerned that your story may be destined for the bin, you can try some trusted ways to turn your pig's ear into a silk purse. A good story is often a package, with a 'Factor X' which lifts it out of the ordinary. Here are some pointers:

Sexing it up

This vile expression entered the language with reference to the government's supposed insistence that intelligence reports into Saddam Hussein's weapons of mass destruction should be stronger, clearer, and more likely to scare the life out of us. It already runs the risk of become overused and meaningless. What it describes, however, is a process in which spin doctors engage every day. If you're campaigning for a cause, or getting your company noticed, or plugging your client's new book or film, you have to sex it up. You have to highlight the exciting, positive, upbeat elements of your message. You have to make it sound interesting and newsworthy. If you don't sound enthusiastic, why should anyone care what you say? George Bernard Shaw once complained that journalists couldn't tell the difference between 'a bicycle accident and the collapse of civilisation' and you should be careful not to wander into hyperbole. But don't sell yourself short either.

Pictures

Even the broadest of broadsheets need dramatic, eye-catching pictures every day. You can use pictures in two ways: first, they can help you tell your story or get a message across in a direct and rapid fashion and second, they can help you sell your story to a publication because the picture is worth publishing. As we have seen from setting up photo-opportunities, a photo must be interesting. This means no men in suits, no novelty cheques, and no handshakes. You can email your picture with your news release. Local papers particularly rely on good pictures being supplied from outside.

Surveys

Have you ever noticed that more surveys are reported in summer and over Christmas than any other time of year? This is because a survey is a good method of creating news from nothing, and when news is thin on the ground, a survey can get your story published or broadcast.

Companies often publish surveys in the field of their business: so a building society will publish a survey on first-time buyers, a pensions company will find out about people's savings, a women's mag will survey women about their favourite designers, and a condom company will survey young people about their attitudes to sex. The same guide to news values applies to survey results – so they need to be shocking, surprising, funny or counter-intuitive.

If your survey shows that men like football, young people use mobile phones, or older people are concerned about crime, then all you can expect is a chorus of 'so what!'

Secrets

News is what someone, somewhere, doesn't want you to know. So if you can persuade the journalist that they are being let in on a secret, your story becomes more newsworthy.

The Advertiser, covering north and east Manchester, reported on 4 February 2005 that Tony Blair had been in town. What made it a front-page story? Here's why:

> **PM IN SECRET VISIT**
>
> The Prime Minister took time out of his busy schedule to meet residents at an early morning meeting in Beswick this week.

Journalists love finding things out that they think they're not supposed to know about. This might involve buying a large ink stamp and stamping the word 'secret' on documents before giving them to journalists.

Stunts

Who's heard of Fathers 4 Justice? Who would have heard of them if their campaign consisted of writing letters, signing petitions, lobbying ministers and waving placards? So how have Fathers 4 Justice achieved such attention? In recent years, this small, impoverished campaign group has made the use of stunts their own. Leaving aside the case they make, and the legality of their methods, few can argue that they haven't been effective in raising their profile.

They've done it by capturing the media's attention in two ways – one, by choosing high-profile target buildings and people, and two, by using humour. It is easy for the media to ignore yet another petition, demonstration, or public meeting. It is impossible for the media to ignore a man dressed as Batman perched on the outside wall of Buckingham Palace, or throwing a condom full of purple powder paint at the Prime Minister during Prime Minister's Questions in the House of Commons. I'm not sure which is more impressive – the audacity of the stunt, or the thrower's accurate aim.

You can use stunts to grab media attention, and you don't have to scale Buckingham Palace. Stunts are events which appeal to the journalists' sense of the unusual or unique. They intrigue and excite the person seeing the stunt in the media. Stunts usually have a purpose – to sell products or to make a point. The Beatles staged a concert on the roof of the Apple Building in central London in 1969, causing traffic chaos and plenty of publicity. The stunt was later copied by the rock band U2.

In 1997 a character known as Swampy became temporarily famous. Swampy and his chums were anti-roads protesters, who would go to extraordinarily dangerous lengths to delay road-building programmes by digging tunnels and concreting themselves into the path of bulldozers. Swampy pulled one of the best stunts of the year by announcing that he would be standing as a candidate in that year's general election. He faxed his hand-scrawled announcement to the newsrooms, and the story hit the headlines. Only afterwards did Swampy reveal that it was a hoax. Perhaps journalists should have spotted two give-away clues: Swampy is an anarchist and an unlikely parliamentary hopeful, and the announcement came on 1 April.

Cedric the Pig became famous in 1995 as the row over privatised utilities' executive pay reached its height. Phil Woolas, then spin doctor for the GMB trade union, introduced Cedric (named after Cedric Brown, chairman of British Gas) to the media – and they loved him. Cedric became the symbol of the 'snouts in the trough' beneficiaries of the Tories' sell-off of state-owned utilities, and appeared all over the television, radio and press. Cedric's retirement even merited a news item on *London Tonight*.

John Prescott donned a wetsuit and aqualung and swam down the Thames to make a point about pollution. The campaigning group Surfers Against Sewage went one further – they used a gigantic 'inflatable poo' to float in the sea at pollution black spots to illustrate their point.

The gay rights group Outrage depend upon daring and attention-grabbing stunts to make their points. Their stunts have included a mass gay 'kiss-in' in Trafalgar Square, and the laying of a wreath to commemorate gay victims of war at the Cenotaph. These stunts cause offence to some, and therefore create a rumpus in the media, which is exactly what Outrage want.

Toy company Mattel, as part of their promotion of the Barbie Doll, arranged for an entire street in Salford, near Manchester, to be painted bright pink. The company promised the residents of Ash Street to give their homes a new coat of paint after a month, and they donated money to community projects. The stunt appeared in the nationals, and on ITN News at Ten.

In 2004 Reg Keys, the father of a military policeman killed in Iraq, climbed a telephone mast outside Labour's conference in Brighton, placed a noose around his neck, and threatened to hang himself. His picture appeared in several newspapers the following morning. Inside the conference, a group of fox-hunters masquerading as Labour Party delegates set off rape alarms as the Prime Minister made his speech. They too won acres of coverage in the papers and on radio and television.

In May 2005, Manchester United fans protesting about the takeover of their club by Malcolm Glazier burnt his effigy outside Old Trafford – and appeared on the television news around the world.

Stunts are for those who don't care too much about the seriousness with which they are treated, or by those – such as campaigning groups – who feel the media will not take any notice if they play by the rules. Use stunts with care – but recognise that they can play an important role in grabbing the media's attention and gaining coverage.

Celebrities

The power of celebrity has been seen when we looked at news values. If you can persuade a celebrity to add their name to your cause, you add newsworthiness to your stories. Even the Labour Party conference in 2004 was made to look interesting and glamorous by the appearance of U2 rock god Bono. He even gave a half-decent speech.

It is important to match the celebrity to the cause, so that the associations people have with your celebrity are the same as you want for your organisation. Charities use celebrities who share their values or have some connection. For example, the Alzheimer's Society is supported by Anne Robinson. A potential problem is when your celebrity becomes embroiled in a scandal, and your organisation is unfairly dragged through the mud.

Celebrities who are trying to sell a book, film or new range of perfume are more willing to take part in publicity events. So are celebrities who are appearing in the local theatre or panto. Your link to celebrity can be tenuous. I once went to a fringe meeting organised by a charity, where the refreshments included 'Ainsley Harriott's fruit punch', made to an alcohol-free recipe specially for the event. A cynic might wonder just how involved the celebrity chef was in creating this drink, but his name appeared supporting the event nonetheless.

When a group of female clergy went to Downing Street in January 2005 to lobby the Prime Minister over world poverty, who better to take with them than the Vicar of Dibley? With Dawn French at their head, the campaigners were met by Tony Blair himself in front of the cameras, and guaranteed acres of coverage. Sad to say, without Dawn French they would have joined the queues of other petitioners and lobbyists, and might have received a few paragraphs in the *Church Times*.

And what about Jamie Oliver and his crusade to improve school lunches? Nutritionists, teachers and parents have been warning about the health effects of feeding school children processed food laden with salt, fat and sugar. But it took a television chef to change government policy.

Exclusives

The word 'exclusive' appears on so many stories, especially in the tabloids, that the term has become devalued. 'Exclusive' means that the story appears in only the newspaper publishing it. Because of the intense rivalry between tabloids, the same story can appear in *The Sun* and the *Mirror* as an 'exclusive'. For the spin doctor, an exclusive is a means of giving a story some extra velocity. If a journalist knows they are getting a story on an exclusive basis, they may give it extra prominence.

A strong exclusive story which appears in *The Times* or *Mirror* will generate immediate coverage in that day's radio and television news, and follow-up coverage in the next day's national newspapers. It is important that exclusives are spread around your target media, so that journalists do not become annoyed at being left out.

If you're concerned that your story is a little dull, and unlikely to get a journalist interested, you should think about how to apply Factor X – a good photo, a stunt or a celebrity, or use an exclusive.

Key points

- You have to understand news values to be able to understand what journalists want.
- Does your story pass the 'so what' test?
- Does it include real people, not merely statistics and decisions?
- Has your story a strong element of conflict, celebrity, danger, novelty, or some other news value?
- Can you spice up your story with 'Factor X'?
- Your story may be worthy – but your job is to make it newsworthy.

Chapter Six
Creating a Strategy

The future is not inevitable. We can influence it, if we know what we want it to be.

Charles Handy

'Strategy' is perhaps the most overused word in modern business. People use it to mean everything from a major document totalling several thousand words to their 'To Do' list on the back of a Post-it note. A strategy is more than a list of thing you are going to do, or a list of suggested tactics. The point of a *strategy* is that it is *strategic* – that means it takes a step back from day-to-day concerns and looks ahead. So a media strategy is more than some news releases, an advertising strategy is more than some posters, and a communications strategy is more than a list of tactics, no matter how sound. I can't tell you how many people I've worked with who describe their newsletter, website and news releases as a 'communications strategy'.

When writing a communications strategy, you can do far worse than to adopt the following template. This has been used by all sorts of organisations, large and small, and it provides a useful starting point:

Communications strategy template
- Objectives
- Targets
- Audiences
- Messages

- Methods, tools and tactics
- Timing
- Resources
- Evaluation

In short, you need to ask yourself:
  - What do I want to achieve?
  - What measurable goals shall I set myself?
  - Who do I need to talk to and listen to?
  - What shall I say?
  - How shall I say it?
  - When shall I start and finish?
  - What have I got to help me?
  - How do I know if I met my ambitions?

What do I want to achieve?

Communications can do two things:
  - it can change people's opinions, and
  - it can change people's behaviour.

If you change the way someone feels about your beans, laptop or holiday resort, they may be more likely to spend their money. If you motivate people about a local hospital closure, they are more likely to vote in an election or sign a petition. So you need to decide: what opinions and behaviour do you want your communications to change?

Why are you spinning? It might be because you want more people to come to visit your restaurant, or buy your cornflakes, or vote for you in the council elections. It might be because you want to get noticed within your firm or organisation. It might be because you want people to be saying certain things about you. It might be – and I pity you if this is the reason – that you want to be famous. Whatever the reason, you must be clear why you doing what you're doing, and what your goals are. There's a useful formula from the world of advertising: AIDA. It stands for:

- Attention
- Interest
- Desire
- Action

Any piece of communications has to achieve each step in the AIDA formula to be successful. You can grab attention by making a big noise. But generating people's interest is harder. Then you have to make people want whatever you're offering. The final part of the formula is hardest of all – they have to take action, be it buying a product, coming to an event, or voting in an election.

What measurable goals shall I set myself?

If you can't measure it, you won't know if it worked. There's a famous acronym from the business world which is helpful here: SMART. Your goals need to be SMART:

S   specific
M   measurable
A   achievable
R   relevant
T   timed

Before setting goals, you need to know about the context, or environment you are operating in. In commercial spin doctoring, that means conducting extensive opinion polling, market research, focus groups, product testing, and surveys. A SWOT analysis lists the strengths, weaknesses, opportunities and threats under separate headings, and helps clarify your thinking. You should be aware of what the opposition are doing and saying.

Even at low levels, you need to work out what obstacles there are to successful spin doctoring. If you want to get your article on hang-gliding into your company staff newsletter to impress the chief executive, make sure they didn't carry an article on that subject last week, or that the chief executive's wife hasn't just broken her legs in a hang-gliding accident.

Who do I need to talk to and listen to?

The key concept in spin doctoring is that there is no such thing as 'the public'. There are instead a series of 'publics' who have to be dealt with differently. You have to decide who your 'target audience' is and communicate with it accordingly. This judgement is one of the most important you will make: your target might be millions of people, it might be just one person. Who do you want to hear your message? People as voters, consumers, or investors? People within your organisation? Your opponents? Your boss?

The idea of different 'publics' comes from marketing and advertising. In advertising campaigns, the target audiences can number millions, for example all females aged 16–24 in social class ABC1. Advertisers segment the potential markets for their products in all kinds of different ways. Here are the main ones:

Demographics (age, sex, race, etc.)
A target audience for a pensions company might be all women and men over 50. A target for a new women's magazine might be all women aged 16–24. You need to know who is consuming what media. For example, *The Times* attracts different types of readers for its broadsheet version and its compact version. Research in 2004 showed that 40 per cent of the readers of the compact were ABC1 aged 25–44, but that was true of only 34 per cent of the broadsheet. Forty-six per cent of the readers of the compact were 25–44 years old, but only 39 per cent of those of the broadsheet. So readers of the compact *Times* are more likely to be young professionals than the broadsheet *Times*, and if that's who you want to reach you need to know that.

Socio-economics

... for example, the National Readership Survey categories of A–B–C1–C2–D–E, in which A equals higher managerial, administrative or professional people, and E equals pensioners, casuals, and the unemployed. These are broad, sweeping categories, and there are exceptions to this rule, for example lottery winners and premiership footballers, but some products can be targeted at managers better than the unemployed.

Geo-demographics

... where social class is cross-referenced with geographical location through systems like ACORN, Pinpoint and Mosaic. Certain postcodes, such as SW6, imply status or wealth, and so those people are more likely to be interested in luxury goods. Postcodes which cover areas with high crime rates might be good for selling car alarms or security systems,

Lifestyle (how, when, why and on what people spent their money)
Some people prefer to buy things from catalogues or over the internet. Some people take four holidays a year. Some people only go to certain shops at Christmas. Some people eat in fancy restaurants once a week. (Who are these people? They sound fun.)

The *Independent on Sunday* (6 February 2005) reported that:

Tories use consumer habits to target voters
The contents of voters' shopping baskets are being studied by both main political parties to help them prepare 'bespoke' campaigns in the coming election.

Labour and Conservative strategists have both bought software that uses hundreds of pieces of commercial and official data to sort Britain's 23 million households into more than 30 specific niche areas.

Whereas Mondeo Man and Worcester Woman became the buzzwords of previous campaigns, this time terms such as

New Urban Colonists and Golden Empty Nesters could join the lexicon.

Psycho-graphics

... which is the study of the attitudes, interests and opinions of people. If someone gives money to an animal welfare charity, they might consider donating to other good causes.

Advertising and marketing are becoming increasingly sophisticated, so that direct mail can pinpoint particular types of consumer. The admen can find out a great deal of information about all of us. Millions of pounds are spent on lists of consumers. A list of consumers who buy wine from a mail-order wine club is worth a fortune to a company wanting to sell luxury foods by mail order. A list of people who eat in restaurants once a week is invaluable for marketing a new restaurant.

In an election campaign the target audiences might be broken down into particular social classes (e.g. 'C2s', 'Essex Man' or 'Worcester Women'), on the basis of how they voted last time and how they intend to vote this time (e.g. 'Tory switchers' and 'Lib Dem waverers') and even at the level of target seats, towns, wards and streets.

In spin doctoring, the market segment can number from the millions to a 'segment of one'. For example, in the 1980s, Tory ministers would fight to appear on the *Today* programme at a certain time. Why? Because they knew that *Today* was one of the few programmes which their leader, Margaret Thatcher, listened to. That was the one person who could hire or fire them who they wanted to reach via the airwaves.

Only when you know who you want to communicate with can you decide how and where to communicate with them.

What shall I say?

What is that you want to say? There is a maxim that all advertising must contain an essential truth – that Volvos are safe, that eggs are good for you, that *The Sun* is fun. They used to sell cigarettes by telling you doctors smoked them, or they were good for your throat. Now, in the light of medical evidence, no one would believe it, so they sell cigarettes on the basis of lifestyle and image. Recent ad campaigns have attempted to tell us that meat and sugar are healthy, despite evidence to the contrary. The ad campaigns that work are ones which tell us something we already believe, or want to believe. The same is true of spin doctoring. The message you want to get across must have at its heart a truth – something that people will believe. All the spin doctoring in the world cannot sell a message that no one believes.

So your message must be believable, or one which people want to believe. It must contain enough truth to pass the plausibility test. The whole of Labour's 1997 election campaign was based on this principle. The promises made (précised on a 'pledge card') were modest and straightforward, and repeated by every candidate and spokesman until we were saying them in our sleep. While some people attacked the pledges for being too timid, no one could accuse Labour of making promises it couldn't deliver.

Staying on message

The message must be repeated and repeated. If you say something a thousand times, on the thousandth time someone, somewhere, is hearing it fresh. The people who are hearing it for a second or third time are having the message reinforced. It is also important to stay 'on message'. This means that if you stray from what you originally said, people might spot the discrepancy and expose you. Within an organisation it means that if the chief executive says that next year will be a successful one for the firm, then everyone else from the head of sales to the cleaner should be saying the same thing.

Japanese companies will spend weeks training lift attendants, receptionists and chauffeurs, not in their actual jobs, but in how to present the company to outsiders. A visitor to a corporation will spend their first vital few minutes of contact, not with a senior executive or smooth PR man, but with the receptionist or lift attendant. In Japan, they can give you facts, figures, and spin about the company, whereas in the UK the likelihood is you'll get a surly temp or jobsworth.

How shall I say it?

As we have seen, the media is a large, complex organism, encapsulating hugely different types of organisations and individuals. You need to decide where you want to see your message appear, and plan accordingly. If you want to reach corporate decision-makers, you might want to target the *Financial Times*, *The Economist*, *Management Today*, *Investors Chronicle* or the finance sections of *The Times* and *Telegraph*. But there would be little point trying to get your story in *The Sun* or the *Mirror* or on daytime TV. During the 2005 general election Tony Blair submitted to interview at the hands of 'little Ant and Dec' on prime-time ITV. He probably reached more voters in 20 minutes than every speech he's ever made to the Labour Party conference in 20 years.

The best way is to draw up a target list of media, and decide how to approach each of them target by target. You need to do some research. This might include reading newspapers and magazines to get an idea of the kinds of stories they print, looking out for the bylines of journalists who write about subjects in your field, or the names of specialist correspondents. It might include listening and watching broadcasters to deconstruct their programmes and spot opportunities.

Drawing up your target list can be made easier by using publications which list all the media in the UK, with their contact details.

The salami approach

From your understanding of the media, you should begin to identify the components of the story, and tailor them to different types of media. Every story can be viewed from different angles, and has different layers. You can slice it up and spread it around.

For example, a syndicate of local government workers wins £2 million on the National Lottery. There are a number of different angles, and different media outlets. On the surface the story is a national news story – the tabloids will be interested to carry the story as a straight piece of feelgood news. The syndicate worked in local government – so the story might provide a little light relief in a serious trade magazine such as the *Local Government Chronicle* or *Municipal Journal.*

The winners all live somewhere – so the local papers, radio and TV will want to cover the story from a local angle. The in-house journal of the council will want to cover the story, as would the magazine of the winners' trade union Unison. There might even be follow-up media opportunities such as features on what it is like to win the lottery, and a good magazine journalist might revisit the winners after a year to write a feature about how they dealt with suddenly being rich.

Every story has these different layers. There is always a local angle if the story concerns a person or place. You can make the local media feed off the national media.

Journalists' most common complaint is being contacted via phone or fax by spin doctors who are contacting the wrong person. Radio stations get sent photographs, the *Manchester Evening News* is emailed a release about a story in Leicester, and the health correspondent is sent a release about a new library. This is a waste of everyone's time, effort and money, which is why targeting is important.

What about how to do it? You need to select the methods which will best fulfil your strategy. In the next chapter we shall look at the pros and cons of different methods.

When shall I start and finish?

We've seen how important deadlines are. Timing is everything. When constructing a strategy you need to build a credible time-frame. Media campaigns need beginnings, middles and ends. Many campaigns have impressive launches, then fizzle out into nothing. A useful device is the Gantt chart, which project planners use to plot activities against time. This means you can see different activities such as news conferences, article publications or photo-opportunities in context with one another. Campaigns are often worked up into a 'grid', showing when events, announcements and media opportunities will take place, designed to avoid clashes and mixed messages.

At the end, you should remember to thank people, send out copies of cuttings, and evaluate your success.

What have I got to help me?

People always assume that the resources they have are their staff and their budget. But often they are ignoring other resources. A community campaign can draw on local experts, volunteers and activists. Most organisations have suppliers, partners and contractors who can help get your message across. Inside most organisations are all kinds of creative people who can help you construct imaginative campaigns.

How do I know if I met my ambitions?

You need to set targets so that you know whether you've been successful.

Spin doctoring is an imprecise activity – it's difficult to measure in any scientific way. You can set obvious strategic goals – such as avoiding a corporate takeover, sending a book to the best-seller lists, or winning an election.

At its most crude, evaluation can be simply measuring the number of column inches in the press and the number of minutes of airtime and adding them up month by month. But that doesn't take any account of the impact of the coverage, the number of readers, the treatment in the editorial, or the positive or negative angle taken. Public relations firms and in-house teams monitor the media and track messages across the media against agreed criteria, for example position on the page, size of headline and so on.

One way of impressing clients is to compare the results of spin doctoring to an advertising equivalent rate – so that an item covering four column inches in *The Sun* would be valued at the cost of buying the same amount of space in *The Sun* as advertising. This is slightly disingenuous as advertising rates are very high, and readers treat editorial differently from advertising.

There are companies which specialise in media monitoring, and can supply you with press cuttings from across the UK, and tapes of broadcasts, based on keywords and subjects which you give them. No matter how broad or narrow your goals, you should set out some targets in advance against which to measure your success, and learn from your failures.

Key points
- Without a plan, you are wasting your time.
- A bunch of tactics and methods is not the same as a strategy.
- Target your audiences like a laser.

- Stay on message throughout the organisation or campaign.
- Have a beginning, middle and end to your media campaign.
- Build in some targets to help you evaluate your success.
- Learn equally from your disasters and triumphs.

Chapter Seven

Spinning in Print

The printing press is either the greatest blessing or the
greatest curse of modern times, one sometimes forgets which.

J. M. Barrie

So what do spin doctors do all day? It's not all PowerPoint and
glamour. There is an endless round of phone calls, tapping the
keyboard, and keeping an eye on journalists. Perhaps the abiding
image of political spin doctors such as Charlie Whelan or Amanda
Platell is of a mobile phone firmly clamped to an ear for several
hours a day. During the 2005 general election I witnessed Alastair
Campbell brief a journalist on his mobile phone whilst at the same
time standing peeing at a urinal. Awesome.

Successful spinning depends on using the right blend of tools
and tactics, from the simple phone call to elaborate and intricate
campaigns.

John Anthony Maltese in *Spin Control,* a study into White
House communications, says:

> Spinning a story involves twisting it to one's advantage, using
> surrogates, press releases, radio actualities, and other friendly
> sources to deliver the line from an angle that puts the story in
> the best possible light. Successful spinning involves getting
> the media to 'play along', by convincing them through
> briefings, backgrounders, or other methods of persuasion,
> that a particular spin to the story is the correct one.
>
> Sometimes the spinner can accomplish the same result not
> by persuading reporters, but by simply making life easy for

them ... briefings and press conferences serve as a watering-hole for packs of journalists in search of news ... well-choreo-graphed photo-opportunities provide striking visual images that reinforce the messages that White House officials want to convey.

'Making life easy for journalists' is perhaps one of the most important techniques a spin doctor can use. There is a range of ways to get your message across. This chapter looks at the main ways of getting your message across in print.

Briefings

A briefing is simply telling journalists information you want to appear in the public domain because it helps your cause. This can be done either on the phone or face to face, and with one journalist or several. A telephone briefing must be conducted at a time when the journalist has no immediate deadline looming. A face-to-face briefing can be done over drinks or a meal, lunch being a favourite. The trick is to have a decent story to give the journalist – they hate having their time wasted, and they may have to justify the time away from the office. If you can throw in some gossip and titbits of information, that will make the encounter more successful. it is a good idea to have a 'leave-behind' – information in written form or on a disc which supports your briefing. In journalism, information is power, and if you can position yourself as a useful source, you will get a good reputation.

News releases

The news release is the bog-standard tool of the spin doctor (it should always be called a news release, not a 'press release', as this excludes broadcasters). It is a document sent from an organisation to a journalist containing a new story, or useful information.

What are news releases for?
The news release is designed to whet a journalist's appetite for more. At the advanced stages of spin doctoring, it becomes less frequently used, when a phone call, a tip-off, or in the case of Peter Mandelson even a slightly raised eyebrow, can make the news.

Given how many millions are produced and pumped out by press offices every year, it is amazing how many are totally rubbish: badly written, wrongly targeted, and destined for the waste bin.

Talk to any journalist and they will tell you the huge proportion of news releases which never get read beyond the first paragraph. Some news releases – addressed to journalists who have died, or to magazines which have gone out of business, or offering photo-opportunities to Red Rose Radio, Preston, don't even get read.

But news releases can be successful, with some thought, skill and effort, and if they follow the rules.

Producing a news release is akin to making a cake. Even with the right ingredients, if they are mixed wrongly, the result is a real mess. If the cake is made correctly, but served as a starter or to someone allergic to icing sugar, it is a failure. Like a cake, a news release must have the right ingredients, mixed in the right order, delivered at the right time, to the right people (and even then, good fortune plays a part).

A news release is geared solely at one audience: the journalist. It has only one purpose: to get the organisation's core messages to target audiences via the media. The issuing of news releases is neither a performance indicator nor the end product of media relations, merely a means to an end. You can write all the news releases you like, but if they always end up in the recycling, you're wasting your time.

The curse of poor spin doctoring, as practised by useless PR people, is to produce news releases which are aimed at pleasing the client. These news releases are characterised by fulsome praise of the client's organisation or product, positioning the client's name in the headline and opening sentence, and splattering the copy with superlatives. For example, it is unlikely that any senior manager of any company in Britain is capable of making an 'epoch-making speech to shareholders' or that any new design of screwdriver is 'revolutionary'.

News releases must contain news

The key to success when writing news releases is to write like the journalist you are targeting. We have seen how news values work, and the sort of stories which appear in the media. The trick is to mould your story into a shape which is recognisable as news.

The upside-down pyramid

News writing differs from writing reports, memos or letters in that the most important information appears at the very start. A report or memorandum may contain vital information in a summary at the end. A news report has the guts of the story in the first few sentences. The way journalists are trained to think about a story is like an upside-down pyramid – with the thickest edge at the top, tailing off to the bottom. As you read down, no new information vital to understanding the story should appear. At the very end, paragraphs might give quotes or added colour and texture, but nothing new. This is for two reasons – firstly, because if a story is edited down to fit a space and some of the final paragraphs are cut, the story still makes sense, and secondly, because not all newspaper readers read every word of every article. The crime of hiding nuggets of information in later paragraphs is called 'burying'.

The Five Ws
Journalists are taught that a story must answer the basic 'five Ws':
– who
– what
– where
– when
– why
We might sensibly add 'how'. Rudyard Kipling, who was a journalist in India, penned a handy rhyme:

> I keep six honest serving men
> (They taught me all I knew);
> Their names are What and Why and When
> And How and Where and Who.

If you look at news articles you can spot the formula at work. A journalist doesn't simply address each 'w' one after the other – the skill in journalism is in deciding which 'w' is the most important and leading with it. This is known as 'the angle' of the story.

The first paragraph from this sad story in the *Sunday Express* (2 January 2005) is a good example:

Boy, 8, dies as gales hit Britain
A boy of eight died as wintry storms lashed Britain yesterday.

– Who? A boy of eight
– What? He died
– Why? Because of wintry storms
– Where? Britain
– When? Yesterday

Or this from *The Sun* (3 January 2005):

ROYAL WEEEE!
The Queen took a tumble at a dinner table – and crash-landed on two corgis, it emerged yesterday.

113

- Who? The Queen
- What? Took a tumble
- Where? At a dinner table
- When? It emerged yesterday

This is from *The Times* (3 January 2005):

> **Fares rise in hope of a better ride**
> Public transport fares rose by as much as 40 per cent yesterday
> as passengers had to pay in advance for improvements to train
> and bus networks.

- What? Public transport fares
- Who? Passengers
- Why? To pay for improvements
- When? Yesterday

This five-W formula is a useful way of analysing the information you have, focusing the story on the strongest news angle, and dishing up the bare bones of the story without any padding or puffery.

The format of news releases

The format must be consistent and meet journalists' expectations of the information they need. News journalists receive hundreds of news releases every day, and can spare just a few seconds in deciding whether to read them or not. The format for news releases must therefore follow the accepted rules of journalism and transmit the necessary information quickly. Obeying these rules of format and structure is the best way to stand a decent chance of your release being read.

Email

If you are sending your news release by email, it is a good idea to put the release in the main body of the email, rather than as an attachment, because most news organisations filter out unsolicited attachments, and most people these days do not open attachments from people they don't know. You can put a logo in the email, and format it to make it look eye-catching. Avoiding spreading viruses is a good plan if you want journalists to work with you.

Paper and spacing

If you're going for the traditional post or fax option, you need to think about the paper. News releases must be produced on news release printed paper, single-sided, with a special continuation sheet. They are produced in 12 point in 1.5 or 2 line spacing, aligned left, with wide margins, perhaps 1" (2.54cm) left and right margins and a 1" top and bottom margin. Wide margins and spacing allow the sub-editors to scribble all over your news release. The release must always be on a single side of paper because journalists will not bother to turn over the page. The top of the release usually has a company or organisation name and logo for swift identification. Journalists will look first to see who is issuing the release, and assess their importance. Larger organisations will put an identification code here, to track their releases. This might be the number and year, like this: PR004/05. This might go at the end of the release. Also, at the top of the release should appear the words 'news release'. This may seem like over-egging the pudding, but it is part of the process of supplying the information in a quickly accessible form for journalists who are dealing with myriad sources of information.

Date or embargo?

At the top left comes the date that the news is issued, or the date and time of the embargo that you wish to place on the information contained in the release. Embargos are used to warn journalists that information issued in advance of an event or announcement cannot be published or transmitted to the public. It is usual for journalists to observe this convention, but if a journalist feels that they can scoop their rivals, and if the source is unimportant enough to risk annoying, they may break the embargo for the sake of the story.

The important thing to understand is that an embargo requests that the journalist doesn't print or broadcast the story, but not that they keep it a secret. I heard of an embargoed news release containing the names of some award winners being sent out from a charity. The journalist phoned the winners ahead of the embargo to see how they felt about winning the award. It was the first they had heard of it.

The convention for news embargoed to a specific day is:

EMBARGO: 00.01hrs Monday 20 June 2005 (one minute past midnight on the day of release.)

This enables newspapers to write the story the day before for appearance on the nation's breakfast tables the following morning. Such an embargo would also allow overnight radio and TV news bulletins and morning radio and TV news to broadcast the story.

Who to contact

Contact details with the name of the person journalists should phone and their contact numbers for 24 hours should appear at the top as well as at the end of a news release. This is to make the process of follow-up as easy as possible for the journalist, and to ensure that if the news release follows on to a second page, the contact details are not separated and lost. It is important that the details are correct, and that the person named has not just gone on holiday. If the named contact intends to be away from the phone, they should brief a colleague so that the call from a journalist is not lost. Ideally the spin doctor should have a mobile or a pager so that journalists can reach them 24 hours a day. News is a 24-hour process, and reporters may well be working on a story late at night, on a Sunday for the Monday editions, and bids for interview may come in early in the morning. Indeed Sunday is a busy day for spin doctors and journalists, preparing for the Monday editions and programmes. Countless opportunities have been lost because a 'contact' was unavailable out-of-hours, and the journalist moved on to another story.

For attention of...

After the contact details comes the name or place the news release is directed towards. So: 'for the attention of housing correspondents' or 'for newsdesks' or 'for the attention of forward planning desks'. This helps get the news release in the right person's hands quickly. If you are not sure who the release should be aimed at, put 'for newsdesks'. It is always best, if possible, to put the name of the actual journalist who will cover the story, which is where building up contacts and researching your target media becomes essential.

Operational note

Occasionally the news release will not contain news, but information relevant to the operations of a newsroom – for example, that a press officer's home phone number has changed, or that a media event's venue has been moved. In these cases, OPERATIONAL NOTE is written above the heading, upper-case, aligned left.

Notice of photo-opportunity

If the news release is an invitation to photographers (sometimes called 'snappers') to attend a photo-opportunity, type NOTICE OF PHOTO-OPPORTUNITY above the heading.

Heading

The heading is bold, centred, usually upper-case, and a maximum of three lines deep (a triple-decker). This is the one element of the release which will almost always be read.

Body text

The body text is the main chunk of text on a news release. It is perhaps 12-point Times aligned left, arranged in short paragraphs, without sub-headings.

More follows or ends

The bottom of the first page must inform the journalist whether there is more on a following page (in which case write 'more follows ...', aligned right, lower-case at the bottom of the page). If the body text has come to an end, let the journalist know: write 'ends', aligned left, lower-case.)

Slug or catchline

At the top of a continuation sheet comes the 'catchline' or 'slug' – telling the journalist that the page is a continuation and identifying the story. The slug is upper-case and preceded by a forward slash, and should reflect the story. So, the first thing on the second page of a news release about youth crime would be /CRIME2, on the third page /CRIME3, etc.

Notes to editors

Notes to editors is a convention whereby extra background information is supplied to journalists. These are numbered, and the first note will always be the same: the explanation of what the organisation is and what it does.

The second note might be information about a spokesperson being available for interview, or that a publication is available on request.

Finally, the news release must end with a contact for more information, with 24-hour contact numbers.

All the of above advice is just guidance – not all news releases coming into a newsroom look identical. But you should try to make all your organisation's news releases follow the same rules, so that journalists feel comfortable with them and know they will contain the information they need. News releases are designed to spoon-feed busy journalists and encourage them to use the information you have sent them. If the news release is difficult to read or if the story is unclear, you have failed.

Some hits and misses (and maybes)
As we have seen, journalists receive hundreds of releases. Here's a small selection sent to the news desk of the *Bradford Telegraph and Argus* a few years ago, and then-reporter Lorraine Eames' judgement of them. The first is from the Imperial Cancer Research Fund.

The headline is:

**Get your church to plant a rose bush for Mother's Day
and Help the Imperial Cancer Research Fund.**

and the intro reads:

> Mothering Sunday will soon be here and the Imperial Cancer
> Research Fund is urging church-goers to join forces to support
> its Mothering Sunday Rose Appeal and help raise money for
> the charity's vital £53 million a year research programme.'

Lorraine says: 'We might follow this up for a picture, but only if a church in our area took part in the appeal'. This one's a maybe.

The next is from the Gas Consumers Council. The headline is:

GCC consumer representations

and the intro runs:

> Today, the Gas Consumers Council (GCC) issues its figures
> for consumer representations during 1997. The council dealt
> with 273,895 representations, of which 44,482 were category
> A complaints.

Lorraine's comment is 'too long and not specific enough to Bradford – I might phone to find any anecdotal information for our area.' Another maybe.

The third, issued by a PR company which ought to know better, is a release about the Guardian Direct Cup, a tennis championship. The headline is

Rusedski christens Battersea Park site

and Lorraine's reaction? 'Completely irrelevant to Bradford'. A miss.

The West Yorkshire Police press office have issued this release:

Making the Most of Neighbourhood Watch'

with the intro:

> A brand new approach is being taken to Neighbourhood Watch as Eccleshill members get together for their annual conference.

Lorraine says this is the most likely to score a hit: 'We'll probably cover this – it's a specific area and a specific event which might be newsworthy. We'll possibly publish something beforehand, and send someone to the meeting.'

A hit!

Clearing news releases
Organisations need a clearance procedure for news releases. This is a necessary process to ensure the release is not incorrect in the technical details, illegal, or untrue. It also provides a second opinion, and to be honest, covers the back of the spin doctor if something goes wrong. If a news release is issued with incorrect data or a mistake, it is conventional for a second release to be issued, putting right the mistake. This is a real pain in the neck, and can be avoided by getting it right first time. The clearance process should

be as non-bureaucratic and as speedy as possible. It is important for the people who are clearing the release to realise that they are checking for factual errors, not altering style. Journalists will not hang around while six different people, who all think they can write, meddle with your news release.

News release checklist
- News releases must contain news, not waffle.
- News releases are aimed at the journalist.
- News releases are short and snappy, and written in the style of the target media.
- The '5W' formula helps you to get to the guts of the story.
- Lead with the strongest angle.
- News releases are not ends, but the means to an end.

Articles

Newspapers and magazines publish articles by outside writers. These are sometimes famous celebrities, columnists, politicians, or the leaders of organisations with something to say. Getting an article published in a national magazine or newspaper can give your cause or campaign a great boost. It makes you look serious and emphasises the fact that your message is worth listening to. So how is it done?

Ellie Levenson is a freelance journalist and journalism lecturer at Goldsmiths College. She writes pieces for *The Independent*, *Guardian*, and *Cosmopolitan*. She says: 'You have to be tenacious, and be prepared to pitch again and again. If you're rejected you have to have a thick skin. Remember, it's the idea that's not right, not you.' She gets ideas from voracious reading of newspapers and magazines. 'I'm not snobby – I read everything from celebrity magazines to broadsheets. Anything can spark an idea. You should be unafraid to write subjects others have covered, because you add a new perspective.'

Reliability is vital. Ellie says: 'If you're asked for 400 words on Wednesday, don't write 800 words on Thursday.'

Many local papers have a 'Soapbox' or 'Your Shout' feature where readers with a strong view are invited to submit articles. Often these slots are hijacked by professional campaigners, but the editors prefer 'real' people with a gripe about a local or topical issue.

Spin doctors are responsible for 'ghosting' articles for their masters. Politicians usually do not have the time or talent to knock out 300-word articles for tabloids on tackling crime, or education standards, so the task is given to their spin doctors. In the late 1990s, Tony Blair's name frequently appeared on articles in *The Sun, Mirror, Express* and *Daily Mail*. You can believe he was a prolific popular journalist during this time, but a more likely explanation is the team of journalists he employed to ghost-write articles for him.

Feature articles' structure and style

Features allow a greater variety of structures and styles than straight news reporting. There is less pressure to start the article with a hard news intro. The intro can use different devices to draw the reader into the article: humour, teasers, questions, shockers, and so on.

You can set up a question to engage the reader, such as in this feature from *Country Life,* September 1995:

> When did you last see, or hear, a skylark?

Try to intrigue or tease the reader, such as this intro from the same magazine:

> Duff House is a thrilling building, made all the more so by its unlikely situation.

Or this from the football mag *Four Four Two:*

> How good is Rio Ferdinand?

Here's the *New Scientist* (December 2005):

> The pilot is counting down over the intercom: 'one minute
> ... 30 seconds ... 20 ...' I am 6 kilometres above the Atlantic
> Ocean and about to lose a lot of weight.'

This is from *Cigar Aficionado* (June 2005):

> Rees Jones is no stranger to dynamite. The award-winning golf
> course architect did such an enormous amount of blasting at
> his stunning Cascata outside Las Vegas that it is said to be the
> most expensive course ever built.

You can start with a historical reference point, such as this intro
from an article about St Helena in *New Statesman* (2 Jan 1998):

> St Helena enjoys one great claim to fame – as the place where
> Napoleon was banished and lived the last six years of his life
> in exile.

You can aim to shock the reader, as Julie Burchill does in an article
in the *Modern Review* (November 1997) calling for censorship of
exploitative images of children:

> There has never been a better time to be a child-molester.

Features about people or interviews might start with a single char-
acteristic. In *George*, (January 1997) the much-missed American
political mag, John Kennedy opened his interview with an ABC
news reporter with the line:

> The first thing you notice about Cokie Roberts, in real life, is
> her eyes ...

'New Lad' magazines can use humour, such as this from December 1997's *FHM*:

> However boring your girlfriend is in bed, you only have to turn on a wildlife documentary to see that there are plenty of other creatures who have a much worse sex life than you.

Or you can try a straightforward scene-setter like this article in February 1998's *GQ* magazine about Newcastle United star Malcolm Macdonald:

> The grey concrete and steel stands of St James's Park steeple up from a hilltop overlooking Newcastle, visible from every direction, like a modern cathedral calling the citizenry to worship.

There are endless varieties of intros, and with practice, you should deploy different ways of hooking the reader into your article.

'Selling in' the article

There's no point writing a beautifully crafted article if no one publishes it. You need to persuade a publication to print it. This process is known as 'selling in' the article. The key target journalist is the features editor, who edits the features section, plans the schedule of articles, commissions writers, and manages in-house writers. This person also has the rotten job of being the target of every genuine freelance, spin doctor, and amateur who thought they'd have a go at writing an article about their trip to Corfu. This means they are every bit as harassed by phone calls, unsolicited articles and faxes as news reporters. They appreciate being dealt with in a professional manner.

Before writing an article you should research your market. Read your target publications carefully. Decide what kinds of articles have been published before. Look at the content, length, tone and style, and emulate it. Write an article which you could easily imagine appearing in your chosen target newspaper or magazine.

Getting your article published is known as 'placing' your article. You can send in your finished article unsolicited ('on spec') to the features editor, but this is unlikely to be successful. It is possible, but a much better way is to seek agreement from the features editor in advance. You should discuss your idea, perhaps with a brief synopsis, with the features editor, and if they like the idea they will commission you to write the article.

It is usual for non-staff contributors to feature pages to be paid, unlike contributors to news pages. The fee should be agreed in advance. Usually there is a standard rate for the job, based on number of words or 'lineage' (number of lines). There might be a 'kill fee' – a payment paid for a commissioned article which isn't actually published.

For working freelance journalists, the point of getting feature articles published is to pay the bills and stop their house contents being repossessed. For the spin doctor, the point is profile-building or opinion-moulding. This means that the issue of payment is very different for journalists than spin doctors. My view is that when spin doctors offer feature material, they should insist on the going rate for the job. That means that the vast PR industry isn't doing journalists out of work, and forcing contribution fees down. You can either keep the cash or give it to charity – it's the principle that counts.

On the other hand, on smaller publications the fact that spin doctors can offer features without requiring payment gives them the edge over other, competing contributors, and might mean the article is more likely to be published. You must let your conscience decide.

Key points

- Newspapers and magazines take articles from outside contributors.

- Target your article to the publication, not the other way round.
- Have something lively and interesting to say.
- Use different styles of introduction.
- Be prepared for rejection.

Other types of article

Book reviews

Most publications carry reviews of forthcoming books, especially in the trade and technical sector, and reviews can be a good way of gaining profile. Publications might have a designated reviews editor, who is inundated with review copies of books from publishing houses and their PR agents. These are sent free in the hope that publications will review them, and the book will receive some publicity. Reviews editors choose their reviewers with care, and try to match the book to the reviewer in a way that will make interesting copy. A biography of a famous politician might be reviewed by another politician who knew him or her well; it might be reviewed by a politician who was their sworn enemy. Either way, the review will have a sharpness and relevance.

Sometimes established or celebrity reviewers can use the review article almost as a comment piece – using the publication of a new book about Ian Botham to write 300 words on the parlous state of English cricket, or the latest edition of Dod's to have a rant about the aristocracy. If you or your boss are attempting to build a profile as a thinker or authority in a particular area, then reviewing books can help establish a reputation. You can phone publishing houses and ask the public relations or marketing section for 'review copies' of books, although they will ask for proof of a commission to write a review, or examples of past reviews. If you can swing such proof of genuine intent, you can get hold of most new books as they are launched.

Obituaries

Obituaries ('obits') are the articles summing up a noted or famous person's life and activities when they die. National newspapers have obituaries already written for everyone in public life, which are updated regularly. Sometimes, as well as the official obituary, shorter obits can appear by people who knew the person well at a particular time or in a particular field. These can be very personal memories or comments, sometimes simply an anecdote which encapsulated the deceased's personality. Obituaries can be submitted to the obituary editor, and can be a fitting way to pay tribute to a respected figure.

Profiles

Profiles are the longer articles about a single person, usually a celebrity, often based on an interview. They tend to appear when celebs have a new book or film to plug. If you or the person you are spinning for gets the opportunity to be the subject of a profile, jump at it. You might even phone the journalist whose name appears under profiles and suggest that they profile you, if you feel interesting enough. These features, always accompanied by a photograph, are the sign that you've arrived, even if it is just in the local paper or trade mag.

A life in the day

feature is a variant on the straightforward profile. Here, a famous person is profiled by concentrating on a typical day in their life, and thus revealing features of their whole life.

My favourite books/year/influences

are the features where individuals are invited to talk about the books they are taking on holiday, the time in their life they were happiest, or the guiding influences in their lives – and by revealing this information, we learn a little more about them. Politicians asked these questions agonise for days over the answers – endeavouring to strike a balance between high-brow and low-brow, between culture and bloke-ishness. The ultimate torture is *Desert Island Discs*, a seemingly innocuous Radio 4 programme which can make or break reputations far more effectively than *Today*. The wrong choice of record (Girls Aloud, say) can end a career faster than you can say WMD.

'Dear Sir' – Letters to the Editor

All publications have a letters page where readers are invited to share their thoughts on the world, comment on things they have read, or sometimes appeal for information. They range from the local paper's letters page to the lofty heights of *The Times,* where sometimes letters from the famous and grand become news stories in themselves.

Some of the letters are from genuine members of the public, some from local dignitaries such as the chairman of the local British Legion, or from national figures like charity chief executives. Some come from letter-writing aficionados like the ubiquitous Keith Flett or Luke Akehurst.

A typical letters page from the *Daily Telegraph* (5 February 2005) comprises ten letters. One is a multi-signatory letter from Conservative women. Three come from campaigning organisations (Action for Prisoners' Families, Dyslexia Institute, Burma Campaign UK), three are from 'experts' (John Yates of the Institute of Historic Building Conservation, Professor Lewis Lesley, and Derek Colley, chairman of governors of St Mary's

Primary School), and three are from members of the public in Norwich, Poole and Rotherham.

Multi-signatory letters, like a petition, are designed to draw attention to some terrible injustice. A group of famous actors might put their name to a letter protesting against the closure of a local rep theatre, or left-leaning types like Tony Benn and Billy Bragg might co-sign a letter about the plight of the East Timorese.

For example, this 'petition letter' from the *Daily Telegraph* (5 February 2005):

> SIR – We believe that any woman who allows herself to be put on an imposed all-woman shortlist – as in the case of the Calder Valley constituency as of today – cannot credibly call herself a Conservative.

The letter is signed by 12 Conservative women, including candidates, 'chairmen', and councillors.

Letters-page editors attempt a balance of 'real' people, the great and the good and people writing on behalf of companies and campaigns. They will also strike a balance between long and short, humorous and serious, and different areas of the country.

Because letters pages are filled with letters from outside, and because a letter can be written and emailed quickly, they are prime targets for the spin doctor.

Here's how to do it:

Take aim …

If you write a letter to your local paper, it will almost certainly be published. Letters-page editors are so desperate that if the letter is in English and organised into sentences it will be printed, even if it makes little sense.

A useful trick is to write a letter on a subject one week, and then have friends ready to write follow-up letters agreeing with you for the following week. You can even 'plant' letters disagreeing with yourself. There's nothing letters-page editors like better than a heated debate.

In the nationals it is much harder to get letters published, as there is greater competition, but even *The Times* has 20 letters to publish six days a week, so you're in with a chance.

In the United States, pressure groups, political parties, lobbyists and even companies have developed networks of people who can be co-ordinated by the spin doctors to deluge newspapers with 'genuine' letters supporting a particular view. The same process is starting in this country. Local Tory associations have been doing it for decades. Lobbyists supporting the roads industry have been known to co-ordinate local residents and community action groups demanding that certain bypasses be built, and ensuring that the message appears in the local papers. Whenever a contentious issue such as abortion or fox-hunting hits the headlines, local papers are inundated with letters from both sides of the debate.

Leading up to the 1997 general election the Labour Party organised a network of letter-writers to pounce on anti-Labour columnists or opinions in national newspapers and magazines such as *New Statesman* and *Tribune*, with remarkable success. A telephone tree was established, and draft points to make were distributed. Although the 'line' emanated from Tony Blair's office, enough Chinese walls were erected to prevent the letter-writers being connected directly with the Labour high command. Over the months, letters appeared time after time, often from different people at the same address, supporting the Labour position.

... fire

A letter to a newspaper usually refers to an article in a recent edition. Usually the article will be a columnist's views, a 'think-piece' or a leader, stating a strong view or position, and the letters referring to the article will take the contrary view. Some can be long, informed and expert views usually disagreeing with what a columnist has said; others can be short, even one line, with a sharp observation or pithy remark.

The letter must contain: your address and daytime telephone number, and the words FOR PUBLICATION at the top. Address it to *Dear Sir*, or just *Sir*, (as in *The Times*).

For example, this typical 'expert' letter in *The Times*:

> Sir, in an interesting article in your series on Victorian Britain ('Conquering disease as an enemy of Empire', August 15) Dr John Snow is referred to as Queen Victoria's obstetrician. In fact he was her anaesthetist; her obstetrician was Sir James Clark ... (*The Times*, 22 August 1997).

This *Guardian* letter (13 December 1997) seeks to put the record straight:

> A journalist of Peter Preston's standing really should know better than to cite that hoary old chestnut about the Inner London Education Authority's having banned competitive team games. This was one of the 'loony left' stories of the early 1980s, ...

In local papers writers, often without giving their names, can have their say:

> I was horrified to hear how many illegal immigrants are being smuggled into our country, which is already over-populated. Is it not time we copied the Americans and issued compulsory identity cards, with our photographs and thumb prints? Then dubious people would not be entitled to obtain money illegally. Dismayed pensioner, Warrington. (*Manchester Evening News*, 8 December 1997)

Or this from the *Evening Standard*:

> At 16 I can buy tobacco and risk dying of cancer. At 18 I can buy alcohol and maybe get cirrhosis, but at 41 I can't buy a T-bone steak. There is something wrong. (9 December 1997)

For the spin doctor the point is not to show how clever you are by knowing the names of Queen Victoria's personal physicians, or that you've just heard the first cuckoo of the year, but to profile your organisation and get your message across. You should be reading the newspapers constantly on the lookout for an opportunity for a letter.

Once you've written your letter, it is usually best to email it to the address listed on the letters page itself, but if you're masquerading as a 'real person', posting it might add authenticity. It should be sent on the same day that the publication appears because 'speed kills'.

Dear Diary …

Diary columns are the light-hearted, amusing columns in newspapers or magazines, filled with gossip and anecdotes, appearing under a pseudonym such as 'Spy' (*The Daily Telegraph*) 'Ephraim Hardcastle' (*Daily Mail*) or 'William Hickey' (*Daily Express*).

Often they take stories designed to plug a new film or book, to advertise an event or raise someone's profile. They can be used to trash someone's reputation, reveal a drunken celebrity's misdemeanours, float rumours too unsubstantiated for proper news pages, or even run vendettas.

If you believe, with Oscar Wilde, that the one thing worse than being talked about is not being talked about, or that even more misleading axiom that all PR is good PR, then diaries are for you.

Each national paper's diary is filled with stories of celebs, politicos, aristos and hacks. Here's a sample from the *Daily Telegraph* (4 February 2005):

Did Howard mean to belittle Alan Duncan?

A story about Tory leader Michael Howard telling a joke about Alan Duncan MP's height.

Patten delivers a handbagging

A story about John Sergeant's new book on Margaret Thatcher and how it got its title.

Faulks's choice: clarinet or sax?

Now that the best-selling author has handed in his latest manuscript, he needs a new hobby.

The dark side of fashion

Katharine Hamnett is launching a new range of menswear.

There are five stories in this edition of Spy, mentioning Michael Howard, Alan Duncan, William Hague, Lord Butler, William Waldegrave, Lady Thatcher, John Sergeant, Chris Patten, Sebastian Faulks, and Katherine Hamnett, in about 600 words. But crucially for the spin doctors who placed some of these stories, there are plugs for magazines, books, and new fashion ranges.

The trick is to get to know a journalist on a diary column personally, develop a bond of trust and establish yourself as a regular source of stories. This will help you to ensure that you don't end up as a diary victim yourself, and if your name appears, it is because you want it to. Providing a flow of diary stories can be a useful source of extra cash – most pay a small amount of cash for a published story. Some establish accounts for regular contributors.

But be warned – if your senior colleagues or famous friends begin to believe that any embarrassing information or private events like naked karaoke will be in the *Evening Standard* by 10 a. m. the next day, then you'll find yourself out of the loop pretty quickly.

And exercise caution: those who live by the diary can die by the diary. Matthew Parris, the *Times* columnist, believes that 'there's a special place in hell' reserved for diary journalists, and they can indeed be malevolent and spiteful. If you use diary columns too much, you may end up as the victim before long.

News conferences
The best advice I can give on whether to hold a news conference is: *don't.*

They're usually more trouble than they're worth, and can be an embarrassing disaster. The first question to ask is: Is the story important enough to warrant a news conference? If the story is major – a new premier league football signing, a resignation from the cabinet, Girls Aloud splitting up (here's hoping), then the amount of media interest will necessitate a news conference. If you are announcing the winner of the local darts league or a change of venue for the retired men's club monthly meeting, forget it. Those spin doctors working in-house, or as consultants, often face pressure from employers or clients who fancy the idea of jostling journalists thrusting mikes into their faces and flashbulbs flashing. Such pressure must be resisted, because there are few more embarrassing situations than an empty news conference. It is the stuff of spin doctors' nightmares.

If you are absolutely sure, then news conferences need to be meticulously planned.

First – choose your venue wisely. To entice journalists away from their desks, it must be convenient for them. A story about rural poverty amongst crofters in the Highlands will not receive much coverage if the news conference in held in a rural crofter's cottage up a mountain. A group of crofters staging a press conference in central Edinburgh or London has a much better chance. The mountain has to come to Mohammed.

So pick a central location near the news centre in your town and region. You can choose a venue because it contains a subtle connotation. When Alastair Campbell was defending himself to the media after the Hutton Inquiry in 2004, he chose the traditional surroundings of the Foreign Press Association in London. He made his statements from the bottom of a sweeping staircase in a building which had once been home to Gladstone. He wanted to reinforce the image of respectability. Some venues imply solid dependability (hotels, institutes, libraries) and others create the impression of innovation (the Institute for Contemporary Art in London, or the Life Centre in Newcastle).

Choose a room large enough to accommodate the expected number of journalists, but not so large that it looks empty even with 20 hacks. If you expect television crews, ensure that there is space near the front for them to set up their equipment, and a power supply nearby. Make sure there is a backdrop with your organisational logo and name. The top table should be covered and uncluttered by cups of coffee and newspapers. It is usually the spin doctor's job to pay attention to the fine detail.

The line-up for press conferences can be a matter of great controversy, as everyone wants to be in the limelight. But the spin doctor must enforce discipline and prevent the top table from looking like a police identity parade.

The best approach is a chair to introduce the speakers, the lead spokesman for the organisation (the chief executive, etc.) to provide the corporate line and an expert (head of research, the author of the report being launched, etc.) to provide factual expert information as a backup.

Photo-opportunities
A picture is worth a thousand words, and part of your spin doctoring may involve using photo-opportunities. Photo-opportunities (or photo-ops) are events staged purely for the benefit of the news cameras, or for photos in-house to be taken and sent out yourself, and used to illustrate a message in a stark visual fashion. These

days, with digital cameras and computer software coming down in price, photo-ops are available to all organisations.

Martin Rosenbaum, in *From Soapbox to Soundbite,* says:

> Photo opportunities work by fostering impressions. They do not assert clear propositions which can be the focus of argument, they establish connotations and communicate subliminally.

For example, during the 1997 general election, Tony Blair made a visit to Dover – a key seat for Labour to win. But the photo-op for the visit, of Blair standing alone against a backdrop of the White Cliffs, had a message far beyond the voters of Dover. The image of a man standing alone against the great symbol of Britain's freedom and independence communicated Labour's messages about Blair being a future great leader, the party's patriotism, and the party's willingness to 'stand up to Europe'.

During the 1983 general election, Margaret Thatcher was photographed in front of the largest Union Jack in the world – on the hangar door of the factory she was visiting. The image – of 'Last Night of the Proms' patriotism – reminded the voters of her victory in the Falklands War the previous year, without a word being said. (Indeed, if Thatcher had tried overtly to use the Falklands War during the campaign, she might have been accused of exploiting the situation.)

Such things can become hackneyed. Lottery winners are usually shown with huge bottles of champagne and beautiful women to show their success. Donors to charity set up photo-ops with oversized cardboard cheques. New buildings are launched by some business executive with a hard hat and trowel laying a brick. Politicians love being photographed with nurses, or babies, or in computer factories.

Business spin doctors run into the problem of making their bosses – grey-suited captains of industry and commerce – look interesting and dynamic. The solution is usually to create photo-ops of these boring-looking men engaged in interesting activities: so, for example, brewery bosses will appear drinking beer.

Some can be even more imaginative. When Virgin boss Richard Branson and radio DJ Chris Evans staged a photo-op to launch their new partnership at Virgin Radio, they invited the snappers in to photograph them both naked from the waist up lying together in bed. The picture was intriguing and memorable, and illustrated the story – that these two big players were 'getting into bed'.

They can backfire – Clare Short's photo-op involving her with landmine-clearing equipment and a 'danger mines' sign caused an outcry, as she was accused of copying Diana, Princess of Wales. In the early 1980s, Margaret Thatcher allowed herself to be photographed alone in an industrial wasteland. The story was supposed to be about industrial regeneration, but instead the photo was used to attack the Tories' record of factory closures and business failures. John Gummer was roundly condemned for force-feeding his daughter a beefburger as a photo-opportunity to prove that British beef was safe.

You should always be aware of potential embarrassments in the background, such as shop names like Booze 'n' Fags, or parts of your slogan on the backdrop which can be cropped to make new words. For example, from certain angles 'Liberal Democrat' can be cropped to say 'rat'. Politicians employ 'advance teams' to recce places they intend to visit and avoid embarrassments.

Journalists are told about photo-opportunities via a type of news release called a 'Notice of Photo-Opportunity'. The basic format is similar to a standard news release, but it is targeted at the photo-desk, not the news desk, and the information contained is the exact time, place, and purpose of the photo-op.

Using a photographer

If you want total control over the photograph, you can commission your own photographs and distribute them to your chosen newspapers, with news releases. This is not a cheap option, but if you have the budget it can be effective.

The same rules apply as for setting up a photo-op: make sure your photograph is fresh, eye-catching and expresses the point of the story. Avoid men in suits shaking hands, groups of people giving the thumbs-up, or over-sized novelty cheques. Try unusual angles, interesting locations, and attention-grabbing set-ups. The human brain, whether male or female, is attracted to beautiful faces (which is why women's magazines have beautiful women on the cover), so use attractive people where possible, without being too obvious or sexist. Use the photographer as a consultant, not merely a technician, because they will have more experience of what makes a good picture and what doesn't.

You should choose your photographer with care. The NUJ *Freelance Directory, Hollis Annual* and local *Yellow Pages* list photographers for hire, but 'photographer' covers a multitude of sins, from local wedding and portrait specialists to famous and rich fashion photographers. You should ascertain whether the photographer specialises in what you want, and always get a price first, including hidden extras like contact sheets, travel expenses, printing and copying. You need to decide whether to commission black and white or colour. This decision is made on the basis of your target media – if you're targeting a glossy magazine, use colour; if it's the local paper, use black and white.

When distributing your photographs, avoid the scatter-gun approach, and try to sell-in the photo to the picture editor over the phone. Offer to email, bike or hand-deliver the photos over for the picture editor to have a look at, rather than describing them over the phone. The less money a publication has, the more likely it is to welcome a photograph. Local papers and trades and technicals cannot afford to have snappers covering every event and so are more likely to use a photograph you send them. Many trade and technical titles carry a section on the people moving jobs or winning awards or contracts in the particular sector or industry, and always welcome simple headshots of the people concerned.

If you have written an article for a publication, offer pictures to illustrate it, and a mug shot of the author to go alongside the byline.

In-house press offices will build up a stock of press photographs of their organisation's leading lights (which, if kept on file for a number of years, can be used to embarrass them at retirement parties), of 'stock shots' of their products or photographs which illustrate their cause or concern. When I worked for the Royal National Institute for Deaf People, we were forever being badgered for pictures of people using sign language or wearing hearing aids.

Key points

- You have plenty of ammunition in your armoury – articles, letters, news conferences and photo-ops.
- Build up a library of photographs.
- Use a variety of tools – don't rely on news releases.

Chapter Eight
Spinning on the Air

Television? No good will come of this device. The word is half Greek and half Latin.

C. P. Scott

Giving interviews

Radio and TV news and current affairs programmes rely on people appearing and saying things. Sometimes this will be highly-paid reporters and presenters, sometimes 'vox pops' of people in the street, but often it will be people representing the view of an organisation or with something interesting to say, known as 'talking heads.' That person could easily be you.

There are two reasons why you might be asked to do an interview. First, because you are the originator of news and the interview is about you, your organisation, your latest report, or whatever. Second, because the news story is about an issue in which you have a direct interest, and you are asked for comment, or expert opinion. The request from broadcast journalists (known as a 'bid') to appear usually comes with only a few hours notice. It often means being in a radio studio at some unearthly hour of the morning, or else in a TV studio late at night.

The programme will try to make the whole experience as easy as possible – they will arrange a car or taxi to take you to the studio and home afterwards, and offer you food and drink when you get there. Some programmes offer a small appearance fee which you can donate to charity, or keep.

Fielding the bid

When the bid comes in, you have to make a snap decision whether or not to take part. Will your appearance help or hinder your cause? Is it a set-up? You need to ascertain key information from the caller (usually a researcher or production assistant):

- What is the programme?
- Is it live or pre-recorded?
- When does it go out?
- Why have they asked you?
- Who else is appearing?
- Has something happened to provoke the story (e.g. a new report you haven't read)?
- How long is the piece?
- Who is conducting the interview?
- What will the line of questioning be?

If the interview is just you and the interviewer it is known as a 'one plus one'. If with you, the interview and someone else, it is a 'one plus two'. The interview may be conducted remotely. On radio, the interview might be conducted over a landline phone, over an ISDN line, or from another studio. If the editor thinks you're worth it, you might end up in a 'radio car' – a kind of mobile studio which comes direct to you.

On television, they might conduct an interview live from another studio or from a location. If the interview is pre-recorded for television, a certain amount of trickery is involved. The crew will only have one camera, so they will film the interviewer asking the questions and nodding at your answers (a 'noddy') separately, and edit it in afterwards.

The most important question is: 'live' or pre-recorded? This information is the most important element of the interview, and changes your whole approach.

A friend of mine was asked to do a local radio interview. He had been told (not by me) that if he made a mistake he should issue a string of swearwords, so that the broadcaster couldn't use the clip, and would have to ask the question again. Having tripped over his words in one answer, he began to turn the air blue with filth that would make a builder blush. Only afterwards did he realise the interview was being broadcast live.

A famous clip of John Prescott involves him doing a TV interview, stopping himself halfway through an answer, complaining that 'that was crap', and then being informed that the interview was live. Both Prescott and interviewer were barely able to contain their laughter.

Most news stories on radio and TV are structured as a debate, because news stories usually contain an element of conflict. One person will make a claim, and an opponent will issue a counter-claim. In a straightforward interview, usually with a politician, the interviewer will articulate the other side of the debate.

The process is best observed on the *Today* programme, the most important radio news programme currently on air, but most news follows the same pattern. A new report from Friends of the Earth will claim that jet skis are dangerous and harmful to the environment. A spokesman from Friends of the Earth will come on the programme and say so, making the case using evidence in the report. Next, a spokesman from the Jet Ski Users Association will refute the evidence of the report, point to jet skiing's perfect safety record, and say the problem has been exaggerated. Your role is to fit into one side of this dialectic, and argue the toss with someone else.

Live interviews can be terrifying – even the most seasoned operators are tested by the likes of Jeremy Paxman or John Humphreys. I've been interviewed by both, and it is a scary experience. The advantage of being interviewed 'live' is that you are in control of the messages you give out. Your words cannot be edited, or juxtaposed with others, or taken out of context.

When the interview is pre-recorded you can take your time to prepare, and get it right. On pre-recorded radio, you will be asked to 'give some level', so the technicians can hear your voice and set their equipment. This is a good opportunity to get used to the microphone, and relax your voice. It's usually a good idea to drink some water just before speaking, because fear will work to dry your mouth.

Despite the perfectly natural pants-wetting terror that appearing on radio and TV induces in most people, and the ever-present danger of making a fool of yourself in front of millions of strangers, there are tried and tested techniques which can help things go smoothly and provide reassurance.

Appearance

If going on TV, appearance matters. On radio, no one can tell what you look like. Television is the most powerful medium, and people tend to remember what interviewees look like, not what they say. That means that smart unassuming business-like clothes and a clean, kempt appearance are essential.

Kennedy is widely assumed to have beaten Nixon in the 1960 presidential election TV debate, not because of policy differences, but because Nixon looked dishevelled, sweaty, unshaven and shifty, and Kennedy wore full make-up and looked smooth and trustworthy. The radio audience, who only *heard* the debate, overwhelmingly voted Nixon the winner.

If you are visiting someone's living room via the TV, the least you can do is look smart. Once I had to appear on *Newsnight* with half an hour's notice, after being tracked down by the BBC in an Indian restaurant in Soho. Without the time to change my clothes, the one feature of the interview that most people mentioned to me afterwards was not what I said, but the fact I was not wearing a shirt and tie. Many spokespeople who might expect bids from television at the last moment keep an ironed white shirt and tie in their office just in case.

TV cameras have difficulty dealing with some bright colours such as scarlet. Small checks and 'dog-tooth' patterns can cause the messy appearance of 'strobing'. I appeared on *Tonight with Adam Boulton* on Sky TV on a panel with a chap whose tweed jacket strobed so badly he had to borrow a jacket from Adam Boulton.

It is normal for men appearing on TV to use make-up – usually some powder to take away shiny foreheads and five-o-clock shadow, and disguise bags under the eyes. In studio interviews, the interviewer is taken to make-up beforehand. In interviews outside at your own location, the TV crew will not have any make-up.

A useful tip for men is to remember to take it off. Straight after my appearance on *Wogan*, I had to get on a train to Manchester. Only when the train pulled into Manchester Piccadilly some three hours later did I realise that I was still wearing full TV face make-up, which explained some of the funny looks from passengers.

If seated for a TV interview, sit on the back of your jacket to stop it riding up and making you look hunch-backed. Straighten your tie. Avoid distracting jewellery, flashy ties or waistcoats. If you want what you have to say to be taken seriously, look sober and respectable, and if you want people to listen to your message, then avoid distractions like wild hand gestures and violent nods of the head.

Body language

Your posture and body language are as important as what you say. You must try (and it is very hard) to control your non-verbal communication. Keep your feet still and avoid the 'foot-flap' – the non-verbal signal for 'I want to get out of here'. Don't shuffle about in your seat, because that makes you look uncomfortable and shifty. Don't close your eyes for longer than a blink, or touch your nose, when answering, because that implies you are lying or have something to cover up. Sit up straight, smile, maintain eye contact, and keep your hands and feet still.

Preparation

Preparation is the key to a successful interview. You must think it through in advance, and practice what you want to say. You should also identify weak spots in your argument, and be prepared to answer hostile questions, although most interviewers are not trying to deliberately trip you up. Write down your key points and rehearse them out loud. The sound of an answer is very different from how it appears on paper.

Ignore the question

The most important technique in dealing with media interviews is to ignore the question. You should decide what you want to say, and say it. The interviewer's question is merely your cue to say your piece.

This technique is nothing new. One of the first British politicians properly to understand the workings of TV was Labour leader Harold Wilson. According to Gerald Kaufman, his then spin doctor, Wilson:

> ... didn't go to the TV studio to answer the questions. The questions were an irrelevance which had to be listened to ...
> he decided what he wanted to say – the message he wanted to communicate to the people who were watching and then, regardless of the questions that were put to him, he said what he meant to say.

Harold Wilson won four general elections.

Similarly, Liberal Democrat peer David Steel admits:

> I always make a habit of writing down three or four points I want to make and proceed to make them regardless of the

questions the erudite interrogators or their even more erudite researchers have made up.

And in the interests of political balance, here's former Tory Prime Minister Edward Heath:

> The thing to do before a big programme is to be clear in your mind about what you want to say, because the interviewer will always try and deal with something else.

Constructing your sound bite

When you have decided what you want to say, you need to condense your thoughts into short, sharp digestible chunks, widely known as 'sound bites'. 'Sound bite' is a term born in the US, and stems particularly from the 1988 presidential election between George Bush and Michael Dukakis. It means the short, snappy and memorable phrase used for radio and TV. The pressures of the media mean that no one gets more 20 or 30 seconds to speak in a news broadcast.

Sound bites are shrinking: it has been estimated that the length has dropped from 40 seconds in the late 1960s to 20–30 seconds by the 1980s. By the 1992 general election, party leaders could expect 22 seconds on the BBC *Nine O'clock News*, and just 16 seconds on ITN's *News at Ten*.

Sound bites have been denounced as undermining and trivialising the political process, by not allowing arguments to be expanded and explained. I disagree. I believe that it is no bad thing if politicians are disciplined into encapsulating their message into understandable, coherent phrases. It helps the democratic process.

Margaret Thatcher says, in *Downing Street Years*, that before winning the 1979 election the Tories had 'taken apprenticeships in advertising and learnt how to put a complex and sophisticated case in direct, clear and simple language'. When a politician fails to properly convey his or her meaning, as Gordon Brown uncharacteristically managed with his phrase 'post-neo-classical endogenous growth theory', they are rightly lampooned. And the sound bite is really only a new version of the slogan, which has been in politics for centuries. Instead of distributing his lengthy political tomes to the Russian masses, Lenin invented a sound bite to encapsulate what the Bolsheviks stood for: 'bread, peace and land'.

During the 1964 general election campaign, Harold Wilson used to judge the moment in his speeches when the BBC would start to broadcast it live, and switch his remarks to messages which he wanted the viewers to hear, not his party-faithful audience.

Your sound bites needn't be candidates for inclusion in the *Oxford Dictionary of Quotations,* but should express your point in a lively and hard-hitting way.

Try and be figurative, without being clichéd. Use visual imagery, if possible, and make statistics come alive with real examples. Be clear what you want to say, and say it. And then keep repeating it like a mantra until the interview is over. You will feel that your interview went in no time at all. That is why it is essential to express your points at the start, because there will be little time to spare. Get your sound bite out into the open immediately, so that the interviewer and other guests must respond to your points, not the other way round. Don't kick yourself in the taxi home when you remember what you meant to say but ran out of time. The French have a phrase for the thing you wish you'd said, seconds after it's too late to say it: *l'esprit de l'escalier*. It's never truer than the moments after the end of an interview.

Beware the pitfalls
Appearing on radio or TV, even on a local station, will have a huge impact. If you do it, you will be surprised how many people comment on your appearance afterwards. You should be keen, therefore, to avoid the pitfalls.

There are the terrible mistakes of the rich and famous to serve as reminders of our own failings. Who can forget George Best appearing drunk on *Wogan*? The lesson here is never to get drunk beforehand (which means avoiding all the free booze in the hospitality suite before going on air).

Never lose your temper (although a good interviewer might try to make you lose your rag; it makes great TV). You should be polite, but firm, and try to get the last word. You should try to use the interviewer's name, but only once (any more and it becomes a distraction or sounds obsequious).

Stay on your guard. John Major's government was dominated by reports of what his Euro-sceptic 'bastards' were up to. The name 'bastards' came from an unguarded remark that Major made to Michael Brunson in 1993 in between TV interviews, while cameras were still transmitting to other broadcasters.

President Ronald Reagan went one better: when asked to speak to provide a sound level check for a radio interview, he announced that the US would start bombing Russia in five minutes' time.

During the 2000 presidential election, George W. Bush whispered to Dick Cheney: 'There's Adam Clymer, major-league asshole from the *New York Times*' in front of a microphone at a rally in Illinois, and the remark was reported around the world.

In May 2005 Prince Charles was recorded muttering under his breath: 'I can't bear that man, I mean he's so awful, he really is' at a photo-call in Klosters after BBC Royal Correspondent Nicholas Witchell asked him a question. His remark became a major story.

Stay calm

Above all, even if you are possessed with the urge to punch the interviewer on the nose, to swear, laugh, vomit, or run out of the studio, you must stay calm. This may take superhuman control if you've had a rough ride from a journalist, or their questions have been particularly obtuse or annoying.

Not everyone succeeds. John Nott, Clare Short and Michael Heseltine have stormed out of studios; Neil Kinnock claimed he wouldn't be 'bloody kebabbed' by an interviewer, and John Prescott lost his temper during the 2005 general election with a *South Wales Argus* journalist whom he told to 'bugger off ... get on your bus, you amateur'. When the journalist threatened to print the remark, the Deputy Prime Minister of Great Britain's immortal response was: 'ooooh ... I'm scared'.

Radio and TV phone-ins
The broadcast equivalent to *Letters to the Editor* is the radio phone-in, which also appears on certain television programmes such as *Election Call* or *Conference Call*. This can be an excellent way of both making your point and putting the programme guest on the spot, or supporting them, depending on your viewpoint. Politicians hate phone-ins because they are unpredictable, and members of the public do not play by the rules of interviewing which presenters usually abide by. A politician who has mastered Jeremy Paxman, Peter Sissons or Kirsty Wark can easily be caught out by a member of the public.

Margaret Thatcher was famously and uncharacteristically caught off guard during the 1983 general election when she appeared on a phone-in on BBC TV's *Nationwide*. A member of the public, Mrs Diana Gould, directly challenged Thatcher over the sinking of the Argentine cruiser *Belgrano* during the previous year's Falklands War. Thatcher was caught out, pressed again and again by Mrs Gould, and came away from the encounter visibly riled. That was the only occasion during the 1983 general election when anyone managed to get the better of her.

US President George Bush (senior) was the victim of a superb piece of spin doctoring in the 1992 presidential elections when he appeared on *Larry King Live*. As Bush appeared to have side-stepped King's and callers' questions on his involvement in the Iran-Contra scandal, a call came in from a 'Mr Stephanopoulos calling from Little Rock, Arkansas'. The call, from Bill Clinton's communications chief, appeared as though he had phoned the public access phone numbers and got lucky. Stephanopoulos, armed with proof of Bush's involvement in arms-for-hostages deals, embarrassed and humiliated the President live on national TV. In reality, the call had been negotiated between the Clinton war room and the *Larry King Live* producer Tammy Haddad, and the stunt hit the front pages the next day.

During the 2005 general election Tony Blair submitted himself to endless phone-ins when teachers, policemen and nurses would challenge his record on the public services. These encounters with 'real people' (as opposed to journalists) provided some spark to an otherwise dull election campaign.

Broadcast interviews dos and don'ts

Do
- Plan what you want to say in advance and rehearse.
- Think in short sound bites.
- Stay calm, relaxed, and comfortable.
- Ignore the question – say what you want to say, regardless of the interviewer.
- Use the interviewer's name – but only once.
- Wear smart clothes on TV (keep a spare jacket, blouse or shirt and tie in reserve).
- Sit on the back of your jacket to stop it riding up.
- Wear make-up (especially for men).
- If possible, men should shave just before appearing.

Don't

- Relax your guard even when the interview is over – sound is still being picked up.
- Look directly at the camera.
- Accept the offers in the green room of free alcoholic drinks.
- Try to be funny.
- Use jargon or technical language.
- Wear distracting clothes or accessories.
- Rustle papers or clank jewellery on the radio.
- Swear, smoke, chew gum.
- Walk out before the end of the interview.

Chapter Nine
Advanced Spinning

From this arises the following question: whether it is
better to be loved than feared or the reverse. The answer is
that one would like to be both the one and the other; but
because it is difficult to combine them, it is far better to be
feared than loved.

Niccolo Machiavelli, 1541

Making complaints

Have you ever noticed that if you are reading a story in a newspaper
about a subject or organisation you know about, it often contains
misspelled names, incorrect facts, and other mistakes? The logic is
that if that's true of the stories you know about, it must also be true
of the stories you don't know about. George Orwell once remarked
that 'early in life I noticed that no event is ever correctly reported in
a newspaper'. In short – newspapers are full of mistakes every day.

What if the journalist's mistake makes you look bad? If you feel
the coverage you have received in the media is unfair, you should
complain. Part of the spin doctors' job is to be on the phone for
much of the day complaining – about perceived bias, lack of time
given to an item, too much time given to an opponent, lack of
prominence given to a story, an interview being dropped, or incorrect or slanted facts.

The process is ongoing. It forms a central part of the continu-
ous process of attrition between spinners and hacks. Some of the
machismo associated with spin doctoring is the ability to pick up

the phone to a respected journalist and attack their work, accuse them of sloppy journalism, threaten to complain to their editor, or freeze them out of the information loop. This bullying, aggressive, downright rude and abusive approach is contrasted with the flattering and charming cajolery which can be deployed when a journalist has done what you want. It also contrasts with the sucking-up that goes on towards media owners and newspaper proprietors by celebs, business leaders and politicians.

The aim, ultimately, is to develop a degree of psychological dependence between the journalist and the spin doctor, so that they know if they're bad, they'll get told off, and if they're good, they'll get a pat on the back.

Occasionally the spin doctor is found out. Alastair Campbell was exposed complaining to BBC TV by fax that their news running order had the verdict in the O. J. Simpson murder trial above Tony Blair's speech to the 1995 Labour Party conference.

In December 1997, the *Today* programme leaked a letter from Labour's David Hill to the editor of the programme, Jon Barton. Hill, then the party's chief media spokesman, wrote to complain about an especially tough John Humphreys grilling of Harriet Harman. The story appeared on the front page of *The Guardian* (13 December 1997) with a full-colour picture of Humphreys under the headline: 'The man Labour wants to gag'. Hill's letter is worth quoting:

> Dear John [sic],
>
> The John Humphreys problem has assumed new proportions after this morning's interview with Harriet Harman. In response, we have had a council of war and are now considering whether, as a party, we will suspend co-operation when you make bids through us for Government Ministers.
>
> Individual Government departments will continue to make their own minds up, but we will now give very careful thought to any bid to us, in order to make sure that your

> listeners are not going to be subjected to a repeat of the ridicu-
> lous exchange this morning … John Humphreys interrupted
> so much that she (Harman) was never permitted to develop a
> single answer. No one seeking to find the Secretary of State's
> explanation would be any the wiser at the end of the 'inter-
> view'. Frankly, none of us feels that this can go on.

Hill goes on to suggest he and Barton 'talk, as this is now serious'.

The leaked letter is an extreme example of the process which takes place day in, day out. Complaining to editors, journalists, even owners, is part of the job. The leaked letter shows that spin doctors, as a last resort, can simply withdraw support from the news creation process, pick up their ball, and go home.

The skill of the spin doctor is understanding who to complain to: when to chastise the journalist responsible, and when to talk to their boss. In his incarnation as Labour's Head of Communications, Peter Mandelson's brilliant reputation stemmed from his under-standing of the news creation process, and his knowledge of the individual journalists working in a particular newsroom on a par-ticular day.

Everyone has the right to complain if you feel you have been misrepresented or unfairly treated. Complaining is a terribly un-British thing to do, and we don't like doing it, but the media can be guilty of terrible acts of unfairness and misrepresentation and they shouldn't be allowed to get away with it.

As Denis MacShane put it in the seminal *Using the Media*:

> Complaining about *bad* media coverage is a vital part of the
> process of getting *good* media coverage.

If a story is incorrect, you should first of all phone the journalist responsible and point out the facts. If the journalist seems unin-terested or hostile, phone up the duty editor. (Don't threaten to go to the editor of *The Times* or the Chairman of the BBC Governors – you'll look silly.) It the dispute is over a matter of pure accuracy such as the wrong name put under a photograph or incorrect figures, the newspaper has a duty to print a correction in the next edition. These will appear as a small paragraph at the bottom of a column, usually titled 'Correction'. For example, here's a correction from June 2005's edition of *Director* magazine:

Correction

Maps of the Middle East published on page 14 of 'Focus on Saudi Arabia' (distributed with *Director* April) failed to name the State of Israel. No offence was intended to any of our readers and we apologise for the error.

Oops!

The Guardian has turned its corrections into a daily item, 'Corrections and Clarifications', and has even published a book of the best ones. Here are some good ones:

On the analysis page, page 13, yesterday we referred to Germany's Italian frontier. It does not have one.

Lord Callaghan's father was a coastguard at Brixham, not Brixton as we said in an article on political dynasties.

On a map on page 13, December 12, the word Cornwall was written across Devon.

We spelt Morecambe, the town in Lancashire, wrong again on page 2, G2, yesterday. We often do.

The absence of corrections yesterday was due to a technical hitch rather than any onset of accuracy.

If your complaint rests on being misquoted, things are less simple. Journalists have the right to use part of what you say, to paraphrase what you say, and to put words into your mouth by asking you to agree with statements they put to you. Naturally, they'll use your quote to accentuate the angle they've taken with their story. A politician might say of a colleague: 'He's a loveable old bastard, and we're the best of friends', but a journalist can report it as: 'Cabinet rift over "bastard" jibe'.

You should try to keep records of exactly what you say – jot down notes as you talk to journalists, because they'll be doing the same thing. Bernard Ingham was famed for his rapid shorthand which meant he had verbatim notes of virtually every conversation he had. At the end of a conversation with a journalist, ask them what quotes they've taken and what they're going to use. You can try and correct them at this early stage if already they're going in an unfavourable direction. If your quote is made up, or gives a meaning entirely different from what you actually meant, you have grounds to complain.

If your complaint is non-factual, and based on a sense of unfairness or distortion, you are on shakier ground, but you should still complain. You might appeal to a sense of fair play and natural justice, or to the news organisation's own producer guidelines, code of conduct, or even the National Union of Journalists' code of conduct. This includes the stipulation that: 'a journalist shall strive to ensure that the information he/she disseminates is fair and accurate, avoids the expression of comment and conjecture as established fact', and 'a journalist shall rectify promptly any harmful inaccuracies, ensure that correction and apologies receive due prominence and afford the right to reply to persons criticised when the issue is of sufficient importance'.

Following the phone call, you should write a letter setting out your complaints. Marshal your case clearly and use rock-solid facts. Copy the letter to the editor or producer. You should try to secure some form of redress – either a printed correction or a guarantee that they will print a letter setting out your case on the 'Letters to the editor' page.

Such a letter can be a good way of setting the record straight (or at least straighter). Here's an example from Gez Sagar, spin doctor for the Millennium Experience, in the *Sunday Telegraph* (28 December 1997): 'Contrary to your front-page report, it is quite wrong to say that the Union flag will not feature in the Millennium Experience at Greenwich ...'; or this, from Anne Fuller of the Magistrates Association in the *Sunday Times* on the same day: 'Contrary to Jonathan Leake's article, Magistrates Association sentencing guidelines have been in use since April ...'.

It is a mistake to take unfair or inaccurate coverage on the chin and think that no one will pay much attention. Today's newspaper is not tomorrow's fish-and-chip wrapper, it is tomorrow's cutting in a file and on the internet for the rest of eternity. A mistake in an article today can resurface years later when a busy or lazy journalist goes through the cuttings file.

Key points

- Complain if you feel you have been unfairly treated: journalists should not be allowed to get away with sloppy writing.
- Today's error can keep on popping up in future articles unless you nail it now.
- Put complaints in writing and stick to the facts.
- Use informal channels first to seek redress, before going to the Press Complaints Commission or the courts.

Dealing with a crisis

Even for the best spin doctor, things can go wrong. Companies can be hit by unexpected disasters such as terrorist action, contamination of their product, or challenges to their safety record. Governments can be rocked by sexual or financial scandals. People within businesses can find themselves on the wrong end of rumours and gossip. In a world where your reputation is your greatest asset, you need to plan ahead to protect it.

The best time to plan for a crisis is when there isn't one, and many large companies keep a 'crisis manual' on the shelf with a set of procedures, and regularly practice them. There are some good books on handling a crisis. Try these:

- *Risk Issues and Crisis Management* by Michael Regester and Judy Larkin (Kogan Page, 2002)
- *The PR Crisis Bible: How to Take Charge of the Media when All Hell Breaks Loose* by Robin Cohn (St Martin's Press, 2002)
- And my favourite (if only for the title): *You'd Better Have a Hose if You Want to Put Out the Fire* by Rene A. Henry (Gollywobbler Productions, 2000)

The key elements are:

What's happening?

First of all, you need all the facts. The crisis team needs to be at the centre of the information flow. All channels of information should be open, and the full picture needs to be established quickly.

Focus the source of information

The worst thing in a crisis is to have journalists getting information from unauthorised sources. If members of staff, eye-witnesses, and various spokespeople are giving different stories, the result will be conflicting information, and you will lose control of the story. In a crisis, there should a single, authoritative and informed source for journalists.

Be honest

Honesty is usually the best policy. If you are at fault, then admit it, and explain what you are doing to put it right. If attempts are made at a cover-up and you are found out, the damage will be much more severe. Journalists will respect and trust the spin doctor who doesn't try to stonewall and gloss over obvious faults.

Take responsibility
The issue of Formula One boss Bernie Ecclestone's donation of £1 million to the Labour Party (and the Labour Government subsequently exempting Formula One from the tobacco advertising ban) is a good example of how a crisis can come from nowhere. The issue became a major news story for days, and marked for many the end of Labour's honeymoon after the 1997 election. The major part of the problem seemed to be that no one had spotted the danger of adverse publicity from Mr Ecclestone's donation and the subsequent decision on tobacco sponsorship, and the story ran out of control. No one seemed to know what was going on. In the end, the Prime Minister appeared in his first full-length television interview since the election to apologise for the affair, and to take personal responsibility. He soon found that this is a tactic you can use only sparingly.

Do something, anything
If something goes wrong, the media will want to know what you are going to do about it, not least to have a further aspect of the story to cover. Being sorry isn't enough. You need to be seen taking action. This might include a full inquiry, compensation for victims, sacking someone, or changing procedures so that it can never happen again.

Be hospitable to journalists
If you find yourself under siege by camera crews and snappers, you will need to create some facilities for them. If they're camped outside your offices, offer toilets and refreshments, a room for interviews and access to electricity points for their laptops. Then sneak out the back door.

Turn the story to your advantage

If things go wrong, there is usually a way of turning the story to your advantage. Don't panic, but instead think how your actions in a crisis might leave a positive lasting image. No one expects the world to run smoothly, and by keeping a clear head and displaying leadership as a crisis breaks, you can earn respect.

Key points

- The time to prepare for a crisis is when there isn't one.
- Keep your crisis plan up to date and regularly test it.
- Shut down unofficial sources of information, and focus journalists' enquiries on a single source.
- Be honest and take responsibility for your mistakes.
- Take action, and be seen to be taking action.
- Turn the story to your advantage – take firm action, launch an inquiry, or sack someone.

Rapid rebuttal

Rapid rebuttal is the technique used in political campaigns when spin doctors are engaged in hand-to-hand combat. It rests on the idea that no claim by the opposition should be allowed to be accepted as the truth. Even at the lowest levels of spin doctoring, the principle of rapid rebuttal applies.

In Labour's pre-Mandelson days, the party would allow the Tories to tell all kinds of lies, and do nothing about it. The rationale was that by responding it gave them a dignity they didn't deserve, and that people wouldn't believe the nonsense put out by Conservative Central Office anyway. Unfortunately, the strategy was flawed because people did believe the nonsense, and if you throw enough mud some of it sticks.

By the 1997 general election, senior Tories couldn't sneeze without Labour putting out a rebuttal. It was an awesome process to watch. No Tory speech, news conference or news release went unchecked. Within hours, sometimes within minutes, journalists would have something in their hands from Labour, putting their side of the argument, disputing the Tories' facts, and pointing out inconsistencies.

Labour's impressive rapid rebuttal was based on a computer database system called Excalibur (Excalibur was the sword of truth in Arthurian legend), which logged thousands of articles, speeches, and news releases. If a Tory candidate said something on pensions, Labour's spin doctors had access within minutes to everything that person had ever said in public on pensions.

Of course, any database is only as good as the people using it. Many of the successes of Labour's rapid rebuttal were because of the humans operating the system, not the computer itself.

The lessons of Labour's rapid rebuttal operation for spin doctors everywhere is that nothing said by your opponents and rivals should ever be allowed to go unchallenged, without your own version of the truth being available. If a lie or distortion is allowed to be accepted, then people may assume it is true, no matter how absurd. That means that someone else is shaping opinion about you, and you have lost control. Some of the lies that Labour failed to tackle in the early 1980s (for example, that Labour councils banned black bin-liners and the nursery rhyme, 'Baa Baa Black Sheep) are still believed by some people. The lies have become accepted as fact.

The obvious extension of rapid rebuttal is 'pre-buttal'. That means getting your argument or point of view into the media bloodstream before your opponents have had their chance.

Dirty tricks

We all know that there are occasions when spin doctors do things that might seem to the casual observer distasteful. In early 2005, the Labour Party was wrapped up in a dirty tricks row for posters depicting the Conservatives' Michael Howard and Oliver Letwin as pigs. Labour was accused of anti-Semitism. Why? Because both politicians are Jewish. But if you unpick the story, not all is as it seems. The posters only ever appeared in emails sent to members, and then reproduced in national newspapers. So Labour gained thousands of pounds worth of 'free' publicity for campaign posters which were never destined for poster-boards anyway. It is significant that the charge of anti-Semitism did not come from Conservative HQ, but from an obscure Tory candidate. So was it really dirty tricks, or a ploy to generate a row to get the posters into the public's consciousness for the cost of an email?

I'm not defending amoral or illegal behaviour, but no book on spin doctoring should ignore some of the dirty stuff that goes on.

Leaks

This is a time-honoured method of getting confidential or restricted information into the hands of journalists. By its very nature, leaking implies that the information has news value: if someone somewhere doesn't want the information released, there must be a good reason why. The technique is simple enough: slip the journalist the material to be leaked in a brown envelope over lunch, or even just post it after a phone-call tipping them off. In the House of Commons the traditional method is to 'leave it on the photocopier' for someone to find. Journalists are honour-bound never to reveal their sources, so if you're caught, it won't have come from them.

Leaks can be used to 'fly a kite' – to see how public opinion reacts to a particular proposal or idea. If the response is rioting in the streets, the proposal can be disowned. They can also be used to steer a public debate in a certain direction. The leak to the *Today* programme of a 'confidential internal MoD report' showing that without extra government funding, the Royal Navy will have no ships by the year 2010 is a good way of winning support for defence expenditure.

The Buckingham Palace spin doctors flew a kite in November 1997 when they tipped journalists off about a plan to open Kensington Palace to the public. They wanted to give the impression of 'modernisation' while also gauging opinion, without having to do anything or make any commitments. Later that year, they tried the same thing with a story about dropping the imperial titles from the honours system. These leaks create the illusion of change and fresh thinking, in tune with popular opinion, and can be denied later if necessary. That's partly the point of a leak – you can inject a story into the news cycle and then refuse to comment on it.

In politics, everything leaks like a sieve. Indeed, as Sir Humphrey puts it in *Yes, Minister*: 'the ship of state is the only ship that leaks from the top'. The difference between leaking and briefing is best elucidated by former Prime Minister, James Callaghan: 'You know the difference between leaking and briefing: leaking is what you do, briefing is what I do.'

Leaks can backfire. When someone leaked advance details of Kenneth Clarke's 1996 Budget and they found their way, via freelance Peter Hounam to the *Mirror*, the editor Piers Morgan gave them back. Perhaps he decided that there was more novelty value in a tabloid editor doing the decent thing rather than simply splashing the leak all over the front page.

Be warned: some organisations employ counter-leaking methods. One way is for each copy of a document to contain an imperceptible and unique form of words or punctuation, so that a stack of what seems like the same document can each be sourced to the recipient.

The stakes can be high if you are caught. In September 1983 a civil servant in the Foreign Office, Sarah Tisdall, was jailed for six months for leaking information about the deployment of Cruise missiles in Britain. Another civil servant, Clive Ponting, was tried at the Old Bailey for leaking details of the sinking of the *Belgrano*.

Spin doctors can use the convention of leaking to their advantage: releasing unpromising material with the added glamour of confidentiality, and making the journalist on the receiving end feel like Woodward or Bernstein, may improve the chances of a hit. The journalist will never know whether the story was genuinely confidential, or destined for release anyway.

Briefing against your enemies

When things turn nasty, some spin doctors brief the media against their enemies. (Enemies should never be confused with opponents. Your opponents are those in rival firms, teams, organisations or parties who are just doing their job in trying to get you. Enemies are the ones who often claim to be your friends. Your enemies are usually 'within'.) The established spin doctor can use his or her trusted relationship with a journalist to do their enemy down: so-and-so is destined for the chop; so-and-so is weak and spineless. It was a spin doctor, using the unattributable briefing as cover, who described Bill Morris in a newspaper as 'pusillanimous', or called Gordon Brown 'psychologically flawed', and another who described John Biffen as a 'semi-detached member of the Government'. Biffen later described Bernard Ingham (for it was he) as the 'sewer, not the sewage' for that particular piece of spin doctoring.

Alastair Campbell, when working for *Today* newspaper, claimed credit for the image of John Major tucking his shirt into his underpants. The image was taken a step further by Steve Bell's cartoons in *The Guardian* which had Major wearing his pants on the outside of his trousers – a sort of anti-superman.

John Major's spin doctor, Sheila Gunn, has claimed responsibility for starting the rumour that Cherie Booth, wife of the PM Tony Blair, had it in for Humphrey the Downing Street cat. When Humphrey went missing from Downing Street, newspapers speculated that Cherie Booth, in a display of Cruella De Ville tendencies, had instructed that the wretched feline be put down. Sheila Gunn told *The Times:* 'it was just one of those ideas that came into my head. It wasn't based on any justification.'

The problem with this kind of briefing is that it debases your cause and makes you look unpleasant. Whatever short-term advantage may be gained is eradicated over the long term.

Misinformation

This really belongs to the world of espionage and conspiracy theory, rather than spin doctoring. The spin doctor is finished if caught deliberately lying to journalists. You can tell some of the truth, even leave information out of the discussion, but to tell a straightforward lie is professional suicide. Black propaganda is the stuff of the KGB, CIA and MI5.

Perhaps the most famous example of misinformation is the Zinoviev letter. The Zinoviev letter (probably forged by the British Secret Service) was the invitation in 1924 from the Soviet leadership to the British working class to start the revolution. It appeared on the front pages of the right-wing newspapers in the week of the October 1924 general election, and undoubtedly cost the Labour Party votes. It is claimed that Major Joseph Ball, an MI5 agent, leaked the forgery to the press. He turned up in 1927 as the communications chief at Conservative Central Office, where he is credited with pioneering many of the early techniques of spin doctoring.

The reds-under-the-beds scare story was still working even after the fall of Communism. In the 1992 general election, the *Sunday Times* ran a front-page story claiming to have unearthed 'Kinnock's

Kremlin connection'. The 'connection' rested on the discovery of a KGB file on Kinnock – no great surprise, as the KGB had files on all the leaders in western democracies, including Margaret Thatcher and Ronald Reagan.

Peter Wright's revelations in *Spycatcher* showed that a group of intelligence officers had sought to malign politicians by starting rumours and spreading misinformation amongst journalists. This included the ludicrous suggestion that Harold Wilson and Edward Heath were Soviet agents, various government ministers were communists, and that Labour leader Hugh Gaitskell was murdered by the KGB. In the lead-up to the 1974 general election Peter Wright claimed that:

> MI5 would arrange for selective details of the intelligence about leading Labour Party figures, but especially Wilson, to be leaked to sympathetic pressmen. Using our contacts in the press and among union officials, word of the material contained in the MI5 files and the fact that Wilson was considered a security risk would be passed around.

Journalist Paul Foot claimed that during the 1970s journalists often took phone calls from 'freelance journalists' offering photographic evidence of Conservative Leader Edward Heath's over-familiarity with young male Swedes, or similar. The photos didn't exist, but the Fleet Street gossip machine would soon spread the smear.

There are any number of malicious rumours doing the rounds about senior figures at any given moment: so-and-so hits his wife, so-and-so is sleeping with his secretary, so-and-so is secretly gay, so-and-so has a drink problem, and on it goes. No one, not even important and powerful people, can be having that much fun for all the rumours to be true.

Turning the rumour mill

Less damaging than outright misinformation is releasing information about yourself so that you get talked about.

Every organisation or social circle has a person who everyone knows is the purveyor of quality gossip. These people set themselves up as the trading post in rumours. They can be used, like any other media. In the House of Commons, reputations can be made or broken by a whip placing a tip-off here or a word in the right ear there, and letting the gossips in the tearoom, sports and social club and members' bars go to work. In companies, people assemble in the canteen, in the smokers' room, by the coffee machine, and what was told in confidence at 9 a.m. will be common currency by 5 p.m.

Try starting a rumour in your organisation, and see how long it takes to come back to you. Tell someone in confidence that you're being headhunted by a rival firm, or that the boss has got you working on a top-secret project, or that you've been asked to draw up a list of colleagues to be promoted or sacked. Then stand back and watch the results.

Spoilers

A spoiler is the device used by rival journalists or spin doctors to undermine, detract or divert attention from a news story. Journalists use it to distract attention from a rival's exclusive story. They either come up with a rival scoop, or simply steal the story and run it themselves. This is possible because first editions of newspapers' front pages are available the afternoon or evening before publication. In central London, you can buy first editions of 'tomorrow's papers' from about 11 p.m. onwards. Newspapers, especially the tabloids, can see what their rivals have done, and spoil it, try to find a new angle, or simply steal it.

Spin doctors use a spoiler to distract attention away from a damaging story about themselves or their masters. In the fevered run-up to the 1992 general election, the *Sunday Times* unearthed some nonsense about then-Labour Leader Neil Kinnock being on KGB files (the implication being that he must somehow be a Soviet 'agent of influence'). As soon as David Hill, Labour's spin-doctor-in-chief, was tipped off about the *Sunday Times*'s intentions to run the spurious 'exclusive' as a front-page lead, 'Kinnock's Kremlin connection', he didn't try and persuade them to stop it. He engaged in the spoiler: he spent his Saturday night phoning all the *Sunday Times*'s rival papers, giving them the story. Thus he destroyed the *Sunday Times*'s hopes of an exclusive and the impact of the story, and ensured that the other papers carried the story with plenty of Labour spin.

During the 1997 Labour Party conference, Peter Mandelson came in for some media flak for remarks he made during a fringe meeting on the minimum wage. As soon as the media pack came hunting for Mandelson, a new, much better story came to light which set them running after a new quarry. An audiotape of Tony Banks describing William Hague as 'a foetus' at the *Tribune* rally suddenly came to light 48 hours after he made the remarks, and the media began a 'Banks gaffes again – should he be sacked?' story. The Mandelson remarks were forgotten. A cynical person might suggest the two events were not entirely unconnected.

The *Daily Telegraph* in February 1998 accused Labour of deliberately floating two 'entirely bogus stories' (about saving the royal yacht, and Chris Patten being investigated for leaking government documents) to deflect media attention away from the semi-scandal of Robin Cook's divorce. A good spin doctor will always have a good spoiler up their sleeve.

It can go wrong, however, as the Football Association's spin doctor Colin Gibson found out in August 2004. Gibson attempted to persuade the *News of the World* to ignore a story about his boss Mark Palios and an alleged affair with FA secretary Faria Alam. How? By giving them an even bigger story about England coach

Sven-Goran Eriksson having an affair with the same woman. The *News of the World* were having none of it, ran the full story, and spin doctor Gibson and FA chief executive Palios both resigned. The FA's reputation is still in the doldrums.

Bribery

There is a growing and unethical form of bribery in journalism which involves linking the publication of editorial material to the placing of advertisements. In other words unscrupulous publications will use your news release, as long as your organisation pays for an advert in the same publication. The coverage is conditional on the payment. This tends to be practised by smaller magazines and local papers.

Another scam is the use of charges for colour separations on photographs. This means the publication will use your photograph, but charge you for the privilege. These forms of bribery damage the relationship between spin doctors and journalists, reducing it to one of simple buying and selling, and also undermine decent standards of journalism.

There is a long-standing tradition of taking journalists on 'site visits' to new holiday resorts, giving them corporate hospitality at sporting events, concerts and the theatre, buying them lunch, and giving them lavish branded freebies. There is no evidence that any of this activity makes any difference to the stories that actually appear in the media.

However, rest assured that large-scale bribery plays no part in spin doctoring, at least in the UK. The spin doctor never needs to resort to such obvious and disreputable tactics because, as the famous words of Humbert Wolfe rightly tell us:

> You cannot hope to bribe or twist
> Thank God, the British journalist.
> But seeing what the man will do
> Unbribed, there's no occasion to.

Key points

- Rapid rebuttal means getting your case into the public domain as fast as possible, before your opponents' arguments become established as fact.
- Pre-buttal means getting your retaliation in first.
- Some spin doctors engage in leaks, spoilers, briefing against others, and creating rumours, but this book does not recommend it!

Conclusion
Into the Light

I sometimes call them the people who live in the dark.
Everything they do is in hiding.

Clare Short MP

We are no more likely to witness the end of spin doctoring than we are to witness the end of rain or sunshine. For as long as there are newspapers, radio and television, and the internet, then there will be people who try to influence what is printed and broadcast.

In August 1996 Clare Short MP famously described the political spin doctors as 'people who live in the dark'. Since the 1990s, political spinners have been dragged from the dark into the media spotlight. Alastair Campbell, Charlie Whelan, Derek Draper, Jo Moore, Martin Sixsmith, Amanda Platell – all these spin doctors have themselves become the subject of news stories. Some, such as Sixsmith and Platell, have sought to use their notoriety to launch alternative careers as journalists, pundits or novelists. Some high-profile casualties have bailed out of political communications. Derek Draper is now a Mayfair-based psychotherapist and Jo Moore is a schoolteacher in north London.

The 1990s was the decade when spin came out of the shadows. What will happen next is that the job of spin doctoring will become better understood, more widespread, and less controversial. In America, the worlds of politics, lobbying, business and show-business are populated with skilled and professional communicators. No one seriously challenges their right to do their jobs, or claims that they undermine American society.

The more transparent and open the process of news creation becomes, the better it is for democracy. The clearer we understand where the news we read, watch and listen to has come from, the better informed we will become. In the future, I hope that no one reads a newspaper or watches a news bulletin in a state of passive receptiveness. The news and views of our newspapers, radio and television should be treated with the same healthy scepticism that we currently reserve for advertising.

All citizens should understand that news comes from certain processes, and is not doled out as a result of unseen forces or magic. We should be querulous and sceptical, and not accept with child-like trust what journalists tell us. Who elected them, anyway?

The more people can influence the media, can make themselves heard, can complain when things go wrong, and can stop journalists stitching them up, the better media we will have. The better the media, the better our democracy becomes.

Glossary of Spin Doctoring Terms

Actuality: sound of an event or an interviewee used on radio.

Advertorial: a paid-for advertisement masquerading as a genuine article in a newspaper, i.e. a blend of advertising and editorial. Advertorials are frowned upon by the Chartered Institute of Public Relations and the National Union of Journalists, but if you've got the budget, don't let that put you off.

Angle: the aspect of a story which you chose to stress, usually one of the **five Ws** (qv). Also known as 'peg' (the thing on which the story hangs).

Aston: the description that appears on the TV screen of a spokesperson or interviewee on TV under their name, designed to let viewers know who you are, e.g. 'Prime Minister', 'Church of England' or 'anti-hunt campaigner'. Named after the Aston machine which makes the words appear.

Back anno, B/A: announcement given by a presenter following the end of a radio item.

Background: part of an article which supplies information to place the story in context. Also information supplied by a spin doctor to a journalist to place a story in context.

Banner: headline on the front page of a newspaper which extends across the full page.

Blog: a 'weblog'. An online diary or running commentary, often written by cranks, egotists or obsessives, with some notable exceptions.

Body text: the main bulk of the text in a newspaper or magazine article, excluding **headlines** (qv), **standfirsts** (qv) or **bylines** (qv).

Broadsheet: large-size newspaper such as *The Guardian* or *Daily Telegraph*. With *The Times* and *Independent* being published in tabloid-size versions, will the broadsheet become a thing of the past?

Bulletin: news programme (UK) or news item (US).

Byline: the name of the journalist who has written the piece when it appears above their article. The byline 'By Our Correspondent' often means the **copy** (qv) has come from a news agency.

Caption: words describing photograph or graphic in a publication, or on the back of a photograph sent to publications.

Cans: jargon for headphones in radio stations.

Case study: what journalists love – real people. A case study is a real example of a person or group of people describing their experiences, and available for journalists to use.

Catchline: the single word used at the top of a news release or copy in a newsroom used to identify the story.

Centre spread: article (usually feature material with photographs) which goes across the middle two pages in a publication.

Clip: a short piece of sound recorded for radio.

Clippings: *see* **cuttings**.

Columnist: journalist (often highly paid) who writes a personal column for publication, setting out their view of current events, what they've been up to that week, which parties they went to, and so on.

Conference: the morning meeting of newsroom staff on a publication or broadcasters to discuss stories for that day's running order or edition of daily newspaper.

Contact: person with useful information or services. For the spin doctor the most useful contacts tend to be journalists.

Copy: written material for publication. Can be editorial copy (news and features) or advertising copy (the text which appears on ads).

Copy flow: the route which **copy** (qv) takes within a news organisation, usually from reporter to sub to section editor to editor. A good spin doctor understands the copy flow within an organisation in order to be able to have influence at different levels.

Crop: to cut a photograph to make it fit the space in a publication, or to create a particular effect.

Crosshead: small heading used to break up a column of text, usually centred.

Cub: a trainee reporter, usually impoverished and eager.

Cuts/cuttings: the library of articles held by news organisations cut from newspapers, stored by person or subject. One journalist friend told me that when he was told by an editor to look something up in 'the cuts', he assumed it was a reference work like *Debretts*.

Deadline: the time by which copy is required. Trying to spin to journalists near deadline annoys them. Trying after deadline is too late.

Diary: humorous, gossipy, trivial column appearing in most newspapers and magazines, filled with tales of the embarrassments and misdemeanours of the great and the good. Usually appears under a nom de plume, although written by a team of writers.

Diary piece: news based on timetabled predictable sources such as news conferences, debates in the House of Commons, business results, football matches, etc.

Down-spin: to play down the importance of a (usually damaging) event or statement. 'That's not important; this really isn't a story …' *See also* **up-spin**.

Down-table subs: *see* **sub-editor**.

Editorial: the column in a newspaper which expresses its own opinion on a matter of importance. Also: all copy in a newspaper that is not advertising material.

Embargo: the time stipulated on a news release before which information cannot be published (but can be acted upon).

Ends: the word that appears at the end of the copy in a news release, to let the journalist know the copy has finished, just before they throw it in the bin.

Exclusive: story given to one news outlet to the exclusion of all the others. Useful tool of spin doctoring, as this creates leverage over how the story is run, and earns credits in the bank with the journalist you give it to.

Feature: longer article (as distinct from news) which covers an issue in greater depth, with more detail and colour, and less constrained by the conventions of news reporting.

Filler: a short article used to fill up space in a publication. The spoof trivial columnist in *Private Eye* is called Polly Filler.

Five Ws: the components of a story: who, what, where, why and when.

Freebie: description of any trip, visit, meal or gift given for nothing, usually to journalists in the hope of favourable coverage or favours.

Freelance: self-employed journalist.

Freesheet: newspaper distributed to readers free.

Ghost-writer: one employed to write articles, letters, even books in the name of another person. Articles in tabloid newspapers by the Prime Minister are a safe bet as examples of ghost-writing.

Green room: the hospitality suite where TV stations offer their interview guests food and drink, in the hope of getting them plastered and making 'great TV'.

Hack: jocular and mildly derisory word for journalist.

House style: set of rules applied to the writing of a publication or organisation, covering accents on foreign words, Americanisms, capitals or lower case, captions, dates, numbers, foreign words, places, names, government and politics, hyphens, initials, italics, jargon, measures, and spelling.

Kill: when an editor decides not to use your article. 'Kill fee' is the contractual agreement to pay a contributor a fee even if the article doesn't appear. Also describes what you want to do to the editor after they've dropped your piece.

Lead-time: the amount of time ahead of publication that a newspaper or magazine needs material by. On major glossy magazines, the lead-time can be months.

Leak: the unauthorised release of confidential material to the media. (Or the pretence of doing so, orchestrated by a spin doctor.)

Literal: spelling or typographical mistake as it appears in written copy. *See also:* **typo**.

Masthead: the title of a newspaper or magazine as it appears on the front page.

mf: more follows. The signal at the bottom right-hand side of a news release that another page follows on.

News agency: news-gathering organisation which sells its news and information to print and broadcast media. National and international agencies (e.g. Press Association, Reuters) serve newsrooms via an online link-up, still known as a **'wire'** (qv) (as in: 'what's running on the wires?')

News conference: event where journalists are given information from an organisation or individual. Usually only used for high-profile news stories.

News desk: the front-line in a news operation, where news, information and tip-offs are first received by reporters and news stories are written.

News release: the short document emailed, posted or faxed to journalists by spin doctors to entice them into covering your story. Most news releases end up in the bin within seconds of receipt. As well as news, can cover operational information and notice of events like **news conferences** (qv) and **photo-opportunities** (qv).

NIB: acronym for News In Brief – the short 20–40 word items of news which appear in columns in newspapers.

Package: a broadcast report made of different components: interview, comment, or music.

Pager: small electronic device which receives short text messages and alerts its owner by bleeping or vibrating. Very nineties.

Panel: the sections of text pulled out of an article (usually attention-grabbing phrases) and placed between two lines, used to break up long articles.

Par: journalists shorthand for paragraph. Sometimes **para.**

Patch: the geographical area covered by a local newspaper or the area covered by a particular journalist.

Photo-opportunities: events staged to provide newspapers with good photographs, which also contain messages from the organisation.

Pre-buttal: getting your rebuttal in first, by anticipating your opponent's next move. *See also* **rapid rebuttal**.

Pre-recorded: term denoting that a radio or television interview is taped in advance of broadcast, and can be subject to editing.

Press Officer: Old-fashioned term for **PRO** (qv).

PRO: Public relations officer (or 'press relations officer'). Junior spin doctor employed by organisation to draft and issue news releases, field calls from journalists, ghost articles for managers, etc.

Press release: *see* **news release**.

Puff: over the top sucking-up to an editor, client, product manu-facturer or your boss in an article or news release. Also: **puffery, puff-piece.**

On spec: when you send an article to the media without prior agreement for publication, in the hope that it will be used (although the chances are it won't).

Op ed: the page in a newspaper opposite the editorial, usually used for longer **think pieces** (qv) and opinion features.

Rapid rebuttal: the doctrine of getting your argument or infor-mation into the media bloodstream as fast as possible before your opponents' line can take hold.

Screamer: newspaper slang for exclamation mark.

Script: a broadcaster's lines.

Sign-off: the name of the journalist who has written the article, when it appears at the end of the text. *See also* **byline** (qv).

Silly season: the period each year around August when most people are on holiday, and therefore there's little hard news. This can be the spin doctor's most fruitful time, because newsrooms are desperate for material. Usually the silly season is when stories appear about crop circles, Elvis sightings, shock survey results, and unfounded speculation about political plots.

Sound bite: the short, snappy phrase used to make a point on radio or TV, usually under 15 seconds long; e.g.: 'tough on crime, tough on the causes of crime'.

Spin control: the influence on the process of news creation exercised by spin doctors.

Spin doctor: if you don't know by now …

Splash: the lead story on the front page of a newspaper.

Spoiler: a news story used by a newspaper to undermine, detract or attract attention away from a rival's story.

Standfirst: the text between the headline and the main text, often used on features and longer news pieces, to draw the reader into the article.

Sub-editor (sub): print journalist who checks and edits spelling, grammar, **house-style** (qv), and length of articles, writes captions for photographs, **panels** (qv) and **standfirsts** (qv) and lays out the page. The sub-editor in charge is called the 'chief sub' and the sub-editor charged with giving the page a final check is the 'stone sub'. The rest of the sub-editors are called 'down-table subs'.

Target audience: the people the spin doctor wants to reach. It might be huge, such as all ABC1s, or it might be a single person: your boss, the week before a salary review.

Think piece: contemplative, longer article tackling a thorny subject (binge drinking, should Britain sign up to the EU constitution, do iPods make you deaf – that kind of thing). So-called because the piece is designed to make you think.

Up-spin: to accentuate the importance of a seemingly unimportant event or statement.

Vox pop: 'voice of the people' interview conducted with members of the public, usually conducted in the street on a particular subject.

Wire: news agency (Press Association, Reuters, or Associated Press) which transmits stories and photographs via computers straight into newsrooms.

WOB: 'white out of black'. Term used to describe a headline reversed out of a black background, for extra visual emphasis.

Working-head: headline on an article used by the journalist to remind them what the story is about.

Select Bibliography

Political spin

Blick, Andrew: *People Who Live in the Dark – The History of the Special Adviser in British Politics* (Politico's, 2004)

Gould, Philip: *The Unfinished Revolution: How the Modernisers Saved the Labour Party* (Abacus, 1999)

Jones, Nicholas: *Soundbites and Spin Doctors* (Cassell, 1995); *Sultans of Spin* (Gollancz, 1999); *The Control Freaks* (Politico's, 2001)

Richards, Paul: *How to Win an Election: The Art of Political Campaigning* (Politico's, 2004)

Journalism

Hicks, Wynford and Tim Holmes: *Sub-editing for Journalists* (Routledge, 2002)

Lloyd, John: *What the Media are Doing to our Politics* (Constable and Robinson, 2004)

Keeble, Richard (ed): *The Newspapers Handbook* (Routledge, 2001)

Public relations

Heywood, Roger: *Manage Your Reputation* (Kogan Page, 2002); *Understanding Public Relations* (McGraw-Hill, 1991)

Hobday, Peter: *Managing the Message* (London House, 2000)

English language

Truss, Lynne: *Eats, Shoots and Leaves* (Profile, 2003)

Evans, Harold: *Essential English* (Pimlico, 2004)

Hicks, Wynford: *English for Journalists* (Routledge, 1998)

Index